SOUTHERN LITERARY STUDIES
Louis D. Rubin, Jr., Editor

ALLEN TATE: A RECOLLECTION

ALLEN TATE

A RECOLLECTION

WALTER SULLIVAN

Louisiana State University Press

Baton Rouge and London

Copyright © 1988
by Louisiana State University Press
All rights reserved
Manufactured in the United States of America

97 96 95 94 93 92 91 90 89 88   1 2 3 4 5

Designer: Albert Crochet
Typeface: Linotron Aster
Typesetter: Focus Graphics, Inc.
Printer: Thomson-Shore, Inc.
Binder: John H. Dekker & Sons, Inc.

Library of Congress Cataloging-in-Publication Data

Sullivan, Walter, 1924–
    Allen Tate : a recollection / Sullivan.
        p.   cm. — (Southern literary studies)
    Includes index.
    ISBN 0-8071-1481-2 (alk. paper)
    1. Tate, Allen, 1899–   —Biography.   2. Authors, American—20th
century—Biography.   3. Fugitives (Group of writers)   4. Sullivan,
Walter, 1924–   —Friends and associates.   I. Title.   II. Series.
PS3539.A74Z89   1988
818'.5209—dc19
[B]   88-6405
                                                                      CIP

To the memory of Allen

Allor si mosse, e io li tenni retro.
—*La Divina Commedia, Inferno I*

CONTENTS

ILLUSTRATIONS

PREFACE

THIS BOOK began with a conversation. One Saturday evening my wife Jane and I lingered at our own dinner table reminding each other of stories not only about Allen Tate, but about other Fugitives as well. We were surprised at how much we remembered, and it occurred to us that what we knew should be written down. It was the kind of idea that comes with the third glass of wine—something to be done some day when you hope you will have more leisure and nothing else in mind to do. But I mentioned the project to Beverly Jarrett of the LSU Press, and by devices that I still do not understand fully, she set me to work. Much of this book belongs to Jane who has done half the remembering and sustained me as always through the agonies that any piece of writing entails. Much of it belongs to Bev too, for her constancy in making me move ahead with the manuscript, and the counsel she gave me along the way. As a matter of decency, most authors thank their editors even when the relationship has been stormy. My expressions of gratitude to Bev are anything but *pro forma*. Along with Jane, she participates in the ownership of this book.

Others have been immensely helpful. Frances and Brainard Cheney—"Fannie" and "Lon"—my dear friends and Jane's, have presided over the Nashville literary community for more than half a century. They were close companions of virtually all of the makers of modern southern literature, most of whom enjoyed their hospitality and many of whom slept under their roof. They share their own memories with uncommon generosity, and I called upon them for aid and guidance many times.

As usual in an endeavor of this sort, there were other helpers too numerous to mention, but here are a few. George Core, who was once my student, has become in many important ways my teacher. He reminded me of some stories about Allen that I had told him years ago and then forgotten; he also read my manuscript and helped to clarify and civilize my prose. Howard Nemerov and Louis D. Rubin, Jr., read the manuscript for the Press. Both suggested revisions that I believe have made the book better. The force of Allen's personality was such that everywhere I went people who had known him were eager to talk about him. Andrew Lytle, Cleanth Brooks, Red and Eleanor Warren, William T. Bandy, and Betty and Monroe Spears are among many who, without realizing that they were doing so, helped me to organize some of my own recollections by going over events in Allen's life that were familiar to us all.

This is not, however, a book based solely on memory. During the time I knew Allen, I kept a journal, much of which was concerned with what Allen did and said. I told him once that I was writing summaries of our conversations and he seemed to be pleased. Though it was not to happen in his lifetime, he wanted someone to write his biography. He had preserved his papers and correspondence, and he was glad, I think, that others were keeping notes.

Finally, my inability to anticipate my deadlines imposed hardships on the secretaries of the Vanderbilt English Department. They are Carolyn Levinson, Florence Muncy, Alberta Martin, and Virginia Schaefer. To them I offer my apologies and my thanks.

NAMES MENTIONED HEREIN

BANDY, WILLIAM T. Authority on Baudelaire and retired Distinguished Professor of French at Vanderbilt.

BARNES, DJUNA (1892–1982). American writer most famous for her novel *Nightwood*.

BELL, MADISON SMARTT. Nashville born novelist and short story writer.

BERRYMAN, JOHN (1914–1972). Poet whom Allen Tate helped bring to the faculty of the University of Minnesota. Winner of Pulitzer Prize, Bollingen Prize, and National Book Award.

BISHOP, JOHN PEALE (1892–1944). Poet and translator whom Allen Tate met in 1925.

BROOKS, CLEANTH. Critic and Gray Professor of Rhetoric emeritus at Yale.

BUFFINGTON, ROBERT. Allen Tate's official biographer who is now in the securities business in Atlanta.

CHENEY, BRAINARD (Lon). Novelist, journalist, advisor to politicians and friend to many writers.

CHENEY, FRANCES. Author, librarian, professor of library science emerita at Peabody College.

CORE, GEORGE. Author and present editor of the *Sewanee Review*.

COWLEY, MALCOLM. Critic, poet, and literary historian.

COXE, LOUIS. Poet and biographer who was visiting professor at the University of Minnesota for 1951/52.

CRANE, HART (1899–1932). Poet who shared a house with Caroline and Allen Tate during the winter of 1925–1926.

CUMMINGS, E. E. (1894–1962). Poet, winner of the Bollingen Prize and the National Book Award.

CURRY, WALTER CLYDE (1887–1967). Longtime professor of English at Vanderbilt and head of the department from 1942 to 1955.

DANIEL, ROBERT (1915–1984). Professor of English at Kenyon who summered at and retired to Sewanee.

DAVIDSON, DONALD (1893–1968). Poet, critic, and political essayist who was both a Fugitive and an Agrarian.

DAVIE, DONALD. English poet and critic who was Mellon Professor of the Humanities at Vanderbilt from 1978 to 1988.

DONOGHUE, DENIS. Irish critic and Henry James Professor of English at New York University.

ELIOT, T. S. (1888–1965). Poet, critic, and playwright.

ELLIOT, WILLIAM YANDELL (1896–1979). Political scientist, Harvard professor, and minor member of the Fugitive group.

ENGLE, PAUL. Poet, novelist, and director of the Iowa Writers' Workshop from 1937 to 1965.

FAIN, JOHN TYREE. Professor of English emeritus at the University of Florida, and coeditor of *The Literary Correspondence of Donald Davidson and Allen Tate*.

FLETCHER, FRANK. Nashville businessman and college friend of Allen Tate.

FERGUSON, FRANCIS (1904–1986). Critic, medievalist, and professor at Princeton until 1981.

FORD, FORD MADOX (1873–1939). English novelist who was a friend of Allen Tate and Caroline Gordon both in France and in the United States.

FRANK, JOSEPH. Critic, scholar, and biographer of Dostoevsky.

FROST, ROBERT (1874–1963). American poet who won the Pulitzer Prize several times.

GARDNER, ISABELLA (1915–1981). Poet and second wife of Allen Tate.

GORDON, CAROLINE (1895–1981). Novelist and first wife of Allen Tate.

GRUMBACH, DORIS. Novelist, critic, journalist, and biographer.

GUERRY, ALEXANDER (1890–1948). Vice-Chancellor of the University of the South when Tate was editor of the *Sewanee Review*.

HARDWICK, ELIZABETH. Critic, essayist, and novelist.

HARRISON, CHARLES (1903–1985). Professor of English at the University of the South. He and his wife Eleanor were next door neighbors to the Tates in Sewanee.

HAUN, MILDRED (1911–1966). Short story writer and Tate's editorial assistant when he edited the *Sewanee Review*.

HAYWARD, JOHN (1905–1965). English editor and bibliographer with whom T. S. Eliot shared an apartment for several years.

HEARD, ALEXANDER. Chancellor of Vanderbilt University from 1963 to 1982.

HEINZ, HELEN. Third wife of Allen Tate.

HOFFMAN, DANIEL. Poet, critic, and professor of English at the University of Pennsylvania.

JARRELL, RANDALL (1914–1965). Poet, critic, novelist, and longtime friend of Allen Tate.

JESSUP, LEE CHENEY. Brainard Cheney's sister from whom the Tates rented a house in Nashville.

JONES, MADISON. Novelist and retired writer-in-residence at Auburn University.

LEWIS, R. W. B. Critic, scholar, and professor of English at Yale.

Loomis, Dorothy Bethurum. Medievalist and professor of English emerita at Connecticut College.

Lowell, Robert (1917–1977). Poet and protege of Allen Tate who won the Pulitzer Prize, the Bollingen Prize, and a National Book Award.

Lytle, Andrew. Novelist, historian, and essayist who for many years was one of Allen Tate's closest friends.

Mabry, Thomas (1903–1968). Short story writer and farmer who was Caroline Gordon's cousin.

Macaulay, Robie. Fiction writer and editor.

MacLeish, Archibald (1892–1982). Poet, dramatist, and critic.

McCarthy, Mary. Fiction writer, journalist, and essayist.

McDowell, David (1918–1985). Editor and publisher.

Maritain, Jacques (1882–1973). French neo-Scholastic philosopher whom Allen Tate met at Princeton. He was Allen's godfather in the Catholic church.

Meredith, William. Poet and friend of Allen Tate.

Mims, Edwin (1872–1959). Head of the Vanderbilt English department during the Fugitive and Agrarian days.

Monk, Samuel (1902–1981). Professor and scholar who served with Allen Tate on the faculty at Southwestern and later urged that Allen be hired by the University of Minnesota.

Nemerov, Howard. Poet, critic, novelist, and winner of the Pulitzer Prize and the National Book Award.

O'Connor, Flannery (1925–1964). Fiction writer who received a National Book Award posthumously for her *Collected Stories* in 1972.

Percy, Walker. Novelist, essayist, and winner of a National Book Award.

Porter, Katherine Anne (1890–1980). Fiction writer and winner of a Pulitzer Prize, a National Book Award, and a gold medal from the National Academy and Institute of Arts and Letters.

POUND, EZRA (1885–1972). American poet who made radio broadcasts for the Italian government during World War II. Tate voted to award him the Bollingen Prize.

POWERS, J. F. Fiction writer who won a National Book Award for his novel, *Morte D'Urban*.

RALSTON, WILLIAM. Anglican priest and assistant editor of the *Sewanee Review* under Andrew Lytle.

RANSOM, HELEN (Forman). John Crowe Ransom's daughter.

RANSOM, JOHN CROWE (1888–1974). Poet, critic, and member of the Fugitive and Agrarian groups.

RUBIN, LOUIS D., JR. Critic, novelist, essayist, editor.

SIMPSON, LEWIS. Critic, historian, Boyd Professor of English emeritus at Louisiana State University, and retired editor of the *Southern Review*.

SMITH, WILLIAM JAY. Critic, poet, and translator.

SPEARS, MONROE. Critic, poet, and one-time editor of the *Sewanee Review*.

SPENDER, STEPHEN. English poet, critic, and memoirist.

SQUIRES, RADCLIFFE. Poet, critic, and biographer of Allen Tate.

STAFFORD, JEAN (1915–1979). Novelist, short story writer, and first wife of Robert Lowell.

STAHLMAN, MILDRED. Physician, expert on diseases of the newborn, and head of the neonatal intensive care unit at Vanderbilt Hospital when the Tate twins were born.

TATE, BENJAMIN ETHAN (1890–1968). Allen's wealthy older brother.

TATE, BENJAMIN LEWIS BOGAN. Allen and Helen Tate's youngest son.

TATE, JOHN ALLEN. Allen and Helen Tate's son.

TATE, MICHAEL (1967–1968). Allen and Helen Tate's son.

TAYLOR, ELEANOR ROSS. Poet who studied under Allen Tate.

TAYLOR, PETER. Fiction writer; winner of a Pulitzer Prize,

the Ritz-Paris Hemmingway Prize, and a gold medal from the National Academy and Institute of Arts and Letters.

WALLER, JAMES (1900–1971). Economist and professor at the University of North Carolina at Chapel Hill. He contributed to *Who Owns America?*

WARREN, ELEANOR CLARK. Writer, winner of National Book Award.

WARREN, ROBERT PENN (Red). Novelist, poet, critic; winner of the Pulitzer Prize, a National Book Award, and the William Dean Howells Medal.

WILLS, JESSE (1899–1977). Nashville businessman who was a member of the Fugitives.

WILSON, EDMUND (1895–1972). Critic and novelist and winner of a gold medal from the National Academy and Institute of Arts and Letters.

WIMSATT, WILLIAM (1907–1975). Critic, scholar, and late professor of English at Yale.

WOOD, ALLEN TATE. Allen's grandson who attended the University of the South.

WOOD, NANCY TATE. Allen's daughter, the only child of Tate and Caroline Gordon.

YOUNG, THOMAS D. Biographer of John Crowe Ransom and Gertrude Conaway Vanderbilt Professor of English emeritus at Vanderbilt.

ALLEN TATE: A RECOLLECTION

ALLEN TATE

A RECOLLECTION

INCREASINGLY, as time passes, there are those who read his work who never knew him. What was he really like? some of them ask, knowing already that he had three wives and two sets of children and many lovers. They have seen his pictures: the young man with receding hair and jutting forehead and full cheeks that dwindled and creased as he grew older. They have heard his voice on records and read some of his letters and the brief accounts that he left of his life: his marriage to Caroline Gordon; his time in New York City and at Patterson with Hart Crane; the year in Paris where he knew Ford Madox Ford and Hemingway and Gertrude Stein; his conversion to Roman Catholicism. Admirers of his poetry know that he was a Fugitive and an Agrarian, a fellow of the American Academy, winner of the Bollingen and of a gold medal from the Dante Society, and that he died in Nashville and was buried at Sewanee beside one of his twin sons. But the facts of his life fail to convey his warmth and his malice, his generosity and his occasional meanness, his enduring capacity to stir people into action and, as likely as not, into controversy wherever he went.

One night, not long before Allen Tate would move back to Nashville for the last time, Lon Cheney pounded on his own dinner table and said, "He's a monster! God damn it, he's a monster! But I love him." Lon was the last of Allen's friends to see him alive. On the final day of his life, Allen was too weak to talk and Lon too deeply moved to risk speech. Allen lifted up his hands. Lon took them. A few hours later Allen was dead. But his capacity for being a cause of disruption did not end until his body was in the ground. His funeral was at St. Henry's Church in Nashville, and he would have liked the ceremony—as well as he could have liked any ritual since Vatican II. The Mass was the Roman Canon, embellished with chants in Latin; there were incense and holy water. The liturgy was as close to that of the church Allen had joined almost thirty years before as it could have been, and in spite of his separation from the sacraments during his marriage to Isabella and much of his marriage to Helen, he had never faltered in his belief and never ceased to think of himself as a Catholic.

After the Mass, the mourners set out for Sewanee. Three pallbearers traveling together stopped for a drink. They stayed too long over their cups, and driving fast in an effort to overtake the cortege, they missed the Sewanee exit and had to go to the foot of the mountain before they could turn around. Those who had found their proper way assembled at the cemetery. There was snow on the ground and a wind and a great sense of awkwardness as people waited around the grave and Allen in his casket waited to be brought there. It was an ending that Allen might have written for himself. Like Wait in Conrad's novel, even in death, he managed to confound the living; and if he could have come back, he would have told the story of the erring pallers with gleeful vituperation. Finally, those present lent a hand; the service was read; the interment was accomplished; the last irony of his earthly days was fulfilled.

I had met Allen for the first time a few miles away and thirty-five years before in Monteagle. Eleanor Ross, who had been Allen's student at Greensboro and was Donald Davidson's graduate assistant at Vanderbilt, asked Allen and Caroline if she could bring me with her to visit them over the Easter weekend. It was April, 1943. I was nineteen, and in July I would go into the Marine Corps. Knowing this, Mr. Davidson had let me come as a sophomore into his advanced writing course. Davidson was the first writer I ever encountered, and I was impressed with him not only because of the poems and books he had published, but because of the other writers he knew and spoke of in class with intimate affection: when he would mention Allen Tate or Red Warren, it was for me as if he had said he knew President Roosevelt, except better, because being a writer was the best thing anybody could be. Now I was going to meet Allen and Caroline, as well as Cal Lowell and Jean Stafford, who were then married and living with the Tates, and Peter Taylor who came from his post at Fort Oglethorpe and Fannie Cheney who also came from Nashville. There were others that weekend, so many that James Waller opened his family's Monteagle house to give everyone a room to sleep in; but I could think only of the writers as we made what was then a tedious trip along narrow roads that began to twist when we reached the mountain.

Eleanor had read all the manuscripts I had submitted to Mr. Davidson. She had told me what stories to bring with me. As we rode she gave them a final perusal and corrected an error in spelling. My euphoria precluded my having any doubts about my amateurish fiction. I did not wonder then, as I have frequently wondered since, whether her last look at my work engendered second thoughts for her about having brought me. If so, they came too late. We arrived at the filling station where the bus stopped and Allen was there waiting for us.

What happened that weekend has no significance in Allen's life. He read my stories, and Caroline read them and discussed them with me, but all I remember is that Allen said one of my titles was too romantic and promised more than the story delivered and Caroline said that my dialogue was too much like Hemingway's. Everybody in the household was writing. Cal and Jean and Allen worked upstairs. Caroline wrote in her and Allen's bedroom, sitting in her robe beside the fireplace and not dressing until midafternoon. At night, Cal would read what he had done that day,

3

which was mostly revisions of the same verses, and Allen, who seemed to have Cal's poetry committed to memory, would comment on even the smallest changes Cal had made.

On Saturday, we went for a walk in the mountains, and that night some of us drank a lot; but others, including Allen and Caroline, went to bed early. The party diminished until there were only four of us left, and we went to the kitchen, which was in the basement, to look for something to eat. We sat around a table talking about literature. Jean asked Peter if he agreed that Cal was the greatest poet who ever lived. When Peter said no, she threw a jar of mayonnaise in his direction. It missed Peter and broke against the wall. This sobered us up, or let us know how drunk we were, so we cleaned up the mayonnaise and went to bed. I do not know what time I went to sleep or how long I slept, but I was awakened by the sound of Allen's making love. My room and that of a female guest who had arrived late that afternoon had once been a single, large room and the partition was thin. I heard the creak of bedsprings and the sounds of passion. Allen's voice and that of the lady were unmistakable; both came to me loudly as they moved toward the culmination.

Decades later, years after Allen's death, I asked Andrew Lytle why he thought Allen had been so determined in his pursuit of women. Waxing more Freudian than before or since, Andrew blamed Allen's mother. "She was a formidable woman," he said. "The sight of her could make Allen turn pale. She could even frighten his brother Ben who was formidable too." Then he said, "Allen wasn't a good lover. I heard him once. He moved slowly and it didn't last long." I do not know how long it lasted on the night I heard him, but for the parties involved, the result seemed to be satisfactory.

To ask why Allen chased women is, in a way, to ask a silly question. People eat because they are hungry, drink because they are thirsty, make love because they are filled with desire. Some libidos are stronger than others; but Allen seemed driven by motives that transcended the satisfaction

4

of the flesh. The woman he made love to that night in Monteagle was handsome. Most men would have been attracted to her, but most married men who intend to stay married try not to be caught in adultery by their wives. Allen and Caroline were to divorce two and a half years later, but to all appearances they were getting along well in April of 1943. On our walk, they had held hands and put their arms around each other. That night Allen left the room where he had been in bed with Caroline, made his passage through the darkened house, and took his pleasure with apparent abandon as if there were no one else nearby to hear.

A paradox of Allen's character, not unique among writers, or humanity in general, I suppose, was that he was deeply sensitive to the emotional needs of others and yet willing to inflict great pain on the women he loved. Did he care whether Caroline knew what he was doing that night in Monteagle? I think he did. I think he would have preferred that she not know, that she not be hurt. But he did not prefer it enough to refrain from doing what he wanted to do, and I believe the risk of her finding out added to his pleasure. Like many other artists, he was bored by quotidian existence. Faulkner said that one of the tragedies of life is that work is the only thing people can do for eight hours straight. But for both him and Allen the problems came when they were not working, when the book or poem or story or essay was finished and they had to wait for the next project to form in their minds. Then Faulkner turned to drink and surliness. Allen turned to controversy and sex and, along with sex, the exciting risk of being discovered.

Except for brief encounters, I did not see Allen and Caroline again until the fall of 1951 after they had remarried. I had a fellowship from the Ford Foundation that required me to investigate ways in which writing was taught in American universities, and this gave me an excuse to visit my friends. Allen was teaching his first semester at Minnesota. He had replaced Red Warren when Red went to Yale, and he told me that he had known how much Red was making and had demanded and got the same pay: $14,000, which was a good salary for those days. He told me also that about a year before the time of our conversation, he had heard a voice inside his mind admonishing him to follow Caroline into the Roman Catholic church, and, of course, he had. Typically, less than six weeks after his confirmation, he had criticized Cardinal Spellman in a letter to the New York *Times*; but when I saw him, he was still euphoric about his conversion, and there was much conversation from him and Caroline, between themselves and to me, about doctrine and practice and bishops and priests. They had priests over for dinner and read J. F. Powers' fiction, and Caroline, who was usually hard on technical cuteness, was delighted with a story Jim had written from the point of view of a rectory cat.

Caroline went frequently to weekday Mass. She would get home about the time I came down to look for breakfast, and, over coffee, she would talk about the church. More directly than any other Catholic I had met, she set out to convert me. She gave me her Father Stedman Missal—her social security number was written in the front of it—and when I remarked without much conviction that I would like to quit smoking, she offered me a saint's medal that had helped her to stop. She took me to St. Mary's where she was teaching and made me talk to her class of pious girls; she put me in the company of nuns who, though less obtrusive in their approach, were as eager as she to make converts. Always, when we arrived at St. Mary's, Caroline would go first to the chapel where, she told me, she prayed daily for the conversion of Lon Cheney, and I suspected that she had begun also to pray for me.

St. Mary's is in St. Paul; going there, we crossed Summit Avenue where Scott Fitzgerald had lived, and we talked of him. I had come to Minneapolis on the train, riding, like Nick Carraway, one of the "murky yellow cars," passing through the "small Wisconsin stations." Caroline and Allen had known the Fitzgeralds in Paris, and she told the sort of stories about Scott's drinking that everybody told who had ever known him. But she found him charming as Allen had, and she seemed now to feel a kinship with him, because although he had ceased to practice his religion long before his death, he had been born and reared a Catholic. At that time, Katherine Anne Porter was still falsely claiming to have been a cradle Catholic, and when Caroline joined the church, Katherine Anne wrote Caroline a disparaging letter that said Catholicism would damage Caroline's fiction. Being a writer herself, Katherine Anne knew that this was the strongest argument she could make; it annoyed Caroline, but she was not swayed by it.

Later, Caroline was to become Flannery O'Connor's good friend and mentor. In the difficult last years of Flannery's life, Caroline said, "Oh, don't worry about Flannery. She's a saint." Caroline also had some saintly qualities. She was strong, and she was as singleminded, as purposeful as any person I have ever known. Even for a novelist, she seemed deeply immersed in her work. One evening, when she was writing *None Shall Look Back*, Randall Jarrell knocked at her door. He had brought along a companion, a figure barely distinguishable in the shadows. "Caroline," Randall said, "this is Braxton Bragg." As Caroline knew, Confederate General Bragg had died before the turn of the century. Jarrell's friend was one of his descendants. But for a moment, Caroline did not think of this explanation or look for any other. It seemed logical to her, obsessed as she was in the Civil War and in her characters who were living through it, that Bragg should be alive too, though history said otherwise. In the instant of her astonishment, she thought of some questions concerning the war that she might ask.

Caroline painted, particularly when she was between books. Her canvases were terrible: portraits that bore scant resemblance to their subjects or to any properly formed human being; landscapes that missed being primitive because they were meant to represent a more sophisticated view of hills and grass and trees. She had few painting skills. Even the simplest exercise in perspective was beyond her.

But she went at every picture as if it were destined for a museum, and she explained the intentions behind her work and the techniques by which she meant to state them to anyone who would listen. She was equally fierce in her literary judgments. She liked Flaubert and Henry James and that part of Joyce's work that Pound described as Flaubertian: the short stories, *A Portrait of the Artist as a Young Man*, and the early sections of *Ulysses*. She did not like Conrad, which I found curious, knowing her devotion to Ford; she said he was "fuzzy." Her judgments were cleanly delineated and well established in her mind, and she proclaimed them with evangelistic certainty.

In the church, she found the ultimate object for her devotion. Without relinquishing any of her loyalty to art, she placed her Catholic obligations above all other responsibilities and callings, and she did not seem to know that the strength of her faith was uncommon and greater than that of Allen or of most other Catholics. Before I went to Minneapolis, I had heard—whether truly or not, I still do not know—that Allen and Caroline had taken, as part of their religious observances, an oath of celibacy. Given his past, this seemed an unlikely discipline for Allen to undertake, but if he did make such a promise, he must have intended to keep it. He knew the commitment he was making when he came into the church. He had read Augustine and Aquinas and many of the other church fathers; he had discussed doctrine and practice with Jacques Maritain, who later was his godfather. Allen was fully aware that implicit in his confirmation was a promise to be faithful to Caroline, and if he believed that he could do that, he might have believed that he could eschew sex altogether.

They slept in separate rooms. They went out frequently. At bedtime, they kissed chastely in the upstairs hall, went to their rooms, and closed their doors—which was almost the only time that Caroline closed hers. As was her custom when I visited her and Allen at Monteagle, she bathed late in the afternoon. She took some joy in going to weekday Mass in her old clothes, an affront to her Protestant upbringing. She painted for most of the day. Then when Allen and I had returned from the university, she would come from the bathroom to her room and spend a lot of time in her underwear. She put on girdle and brassiere, shoes and stockings; then with the door to her room open and going often through the hall to the bathroom and back, she fixed her hair and put on her makeup before she put on her slip and dress.

When I passed her room or met her in the hall, it occurred to me that if they had agreed to live in celibacy, she was not making it easy for Allen. Then I thought that perhaps this was the point: to punish him for all of his past transgressions. But to say this makes Caroline seem vindictive and foolish and she was neither. She knew Allen's nature well enough. But her conversion had made such a radical change in her life, and her own faith was so deep that she could not conceive that Allen's confirmation had not changed his character more deeply. Or perhaps—and this is most likely— they had not undertaken the extraordinary discipline that gossip claimed for them.

I stayed with Caroline and Allen for three weeks. One of Caroline's talents was to be minimally inconvenienced by her guests. I had a room, and if food were to be served, there was a plate for me. But I got my own breakfast, and most other meals we ate out. Allen worked in the morning. At noon, he and I would go to a restaurant near the campus where we would meet some of his colleagues, have lunch and go to his classes. He taught modern literature to a large group of mostly undergraduates and a seminar that also was focused on the twentieth century. Even that first year of his residence, his lectures on Hart Crane attracted many auditors: in subsequent semesters, when he talked about Crane, the class would meet in a larger room to accommodate visitors.

A day or two after I had arrived in Minneapolis, Allen told me on the way to the university that I would have to talk to his seminar. He had just come from an appointment with the IRS at which an agent had told him that he owed $400 in

In the 1930s.
Courtesy Photographic Archives, Vanderbilt University.

Circa 1950.
*Photo by Hans Namuth, Courtesy Photographic Archives,
Vanderbilt University.*

Reading at Vanderbilt, 1956.
Courtesy Photographic Archives, Vanderbilt University.

In the late 1960s.
Courtesy Photographic Archives, Vanderbilt University.

On the Vanderbilt campus, 1967, when Tate was
teaching there for a semester.
Courtesy Photographic Archives, Vanderbilt University.

In the study at his house in Sewanee, early 1970s.
Courtesy Photographic Archives, Vanderbilt University.

back taxes. He thought, probably with justification, that he had been treated rudely by a tax collector who had threatened to put a lien on his car if he did not pay on the spot. "Walter," he said, "I'm too upset to deal with a class. You'll have to talk to them."

"Good God," I replied. "About what?"

For a while he did not answer. We were riding in the car the IRS had threatened to seize, for which, though he was not driving it very well, Allen seemed to have developed an increased affection. He kept patting the steering wheel and muttering, "My automobile. Take my automobile."

"What do you want me to talk about?" I asked again.

"Anything."

It crossed my mind to say Hart Crane, but I was too frightened to joke. "What's the class working on?"

"Four hundred dollars," he said. "Pay today or lose my car. . . . We're on Faulkner."

I was lucky. My last year at Iowa, I had written a not very good paper on *Absalom, Absalom!*. I had recently revised it, and though my revision had not turned it into a first rate essay, it was good enough to be published later. At the moment the material was fresh in my mind. I discussed tragic elements in the novel: Sutpen and Aristotle, Sutpen and Hegel. I didn't do a very good job, but graduate students are so perseveringly intellectual that they will put up with almost anything, and Allen was sufficiently diverted to get his mind off his back taxes and the IRS. When I had run down, he talked about *Absalom* and about Faulkner in general. Then we went home where he fixed us each a martini, set up his stand, got out his music, and played his violin.

The Tates had frequent visitors. Sam Monk came more often than anyone else and on arrival, he hugged and kissed Caroline with more enthusiasm than she thought the occasions warranted. She and Allen had known Sam at Southwestern in Memphis just before or after his wife died. She had drowned. Although Sam had been present, he was not able to save her. His grief had been profound, he still felt deprived and lonely, and Caroline was patient with him. Leonard Unger came and so did Louis Coxe. Raissa and Jacques Maritain had just translated "Ode to the Confederate Dead" into French, and without revealing what it was, Allen began to read the translation saying, "See how you like this, Louis."

After hearing a few lines, Coxe said, "So far, so good, but I'm waiting till you get to that serpent in the mulberry bush."

One evening, Allen and Caroline and I went to a party given by one of Allen's colleagues. Among the guests was a painter who was smaller even than Allen and who was drunk when we arrived: he was accompanied by his wife, a very large woman with enormous breasts. They addressed each other and referred to each other as Mama and Son of a Bitch. After the party had gone on for a while, these were the names that everybody called them. Son of a Bitch went to sleep in Mama's arms and had a long nap. When he awakened, I was speaking. "Wait," he said. "Be quiet, everybody. Listen to the way that man talks."

Everybody fell silent.

"Talk," Son of a Bitch said, looking at me. "Say something."

I felt like Pip being commanded to play. Momentarily, I was speechless.

"Talk," Son of a Bitch insisted.

I managed to utter a sentence or two.

"Listen to how funny he sounds."

Allen bristled. "Do you think he talks funny?"

"Yes."

"Well, we think you talk funny," Allen said.

Son of a Bitch, who had told us earlier that he was from Michigan, was astounded. "You think *I* talk funny?"

"Yes," Allen said, "we do."

"No!" Son of a Bitch said, his astonishment deepening.

"Oh, yes," Allen replied.

17

Allen puffed on his cigarette and looked around the room. Then he said, "Son of a Bitch thinks he talks according to nature."

One afternoon, near the end of my visit, Allen had business to attend to, and I sat in the studio with Caroline while she painted. She was working on a picture of Saint Cuthbert who, according to legend, spent many nocturnal hours praying while standing up to his armpits in the Irish Sea. When he came out of the cold water, two otters dried his feet with their fur and licked them until they were warm. Caroline had gone to a natural history museum in Minneapolis in search of models for the otters and had caused as much consternation with her accent as, a few nights earlier, I had with mine. The woman at the museum thought she was saying *auto* and suggested that Caroline simply look on the street. When finally Caroline made herself understood, the woman said, "Well, we all speak English, don't we?" Caroline thought the exchange had been funny. She had seen her otters, and now she worked in good humor and talked about art and literature. She was criticizing a manuscript by Walker Percy and, she said, charging him good money for it—$250, as I recall. She liked Walker's book and saw in its Catholic foundations what she conceived to be the future of the novel. She compared Walker and Flannery O'Connor, whose manuscripts she had also been reading recently, to earlier southern novelists whose views had been Protestant, of whom she had been one. She began to speak of her own past.

By now her mother was dead, and Nancy Tate was married and had children of her own. But Caroline was remembering the fall of 1925 when Mrs. Gordon came to New York to see her new granddaughter. "She didn't understand why we lived the way we did," Caroline said. "She didn't know how poor we were, and I was ashamed to tell her. She thought I was a bad housekeeper. She would look in the kitchen and find almost nothing to eat, and she thought I was too much involved in my writing to take the time to buy groceries. She lectured me about the proper way to run a house. Then when she discovered that I wasn't buying food because I didn't have the money to buy it with, she took Nancy back to Kentucky."

Later, in a voice slightly abstracted, as though she were speaking to herself, she said, "Our life might have been easier if it hadn't been for Dr. Mims." Edwin Mims was the head of the Vanderbilt English department during the Fugitive and Agrarian days, and he had opposed both movements. He was a scholar of the old school and an apostle of the New South. Years before Allen enrolled at Vanderbilt, Mims had been to the Chicago World's Fair, and the scientific marvels he observed there convinced him that America was poised at the edge of utopian fulfillment. He put his faith in the doctrines of material progress and the perfectibility of human nature. The critical theories that the Fugitives were developing and the opposition of the Agrarians to the industrialization of the South were anathema to him. Even though he tolerated Ransom and Davidson on his faculty, he struck back when he could.

According to Caroline, Allen, during his senior year at Vanderbilt, had applied for and received a fellowship in the English department at Yale. Not even his own self-interest could deter Allen's characteristic impulse toward confrontation and dispute. With the announcement of his award in hand, he called on Mims. "Dr. Mims," he said, "I came by to tell you that I have a fellowship in the Yale English department for next year." Before Mims could reply, Allen added, "And I wanted to point out that I got it without any recommendation from you."

Mims was quick to get revenge. He used his considerable influence in academic circles to have Allen's fellowship revoked. "If Allen had had an advanced degree, he might have got work teaching," Caroline said. "As it was, we went hungry part of the time."

The next day, I repeated Caroline's story to Allen. "Yes," he said. "And Mims did the same sort of thing to Red." In addition to his duties at Vanderbilt, Mims taught a course in writing at Watkins Institute, which offered night classes in general education. The year Red Warren was graduated from Vanderbilt, Mims resigned his position at Watkins and Red, who was as poor as the Tates at the time, applied for and got the job Mims had relinquished. When Mims learned that Red was to be his successor, he rescinded his resignation and kept the job for himself. "He didn't want the work," Allen said, "and he didn't need the money. He was willing to inconvenience himself to hurt Red."

Mims was still alive in 1954 when Allen gave a reading at Vanderbilt. He had long ago been forced to retire, but he spent a good deal of his time loitering around the English department, and when a group of us took Allen to lunch, Mims came too. Afterwards, driving back to the campus, there were six in one car—Davidson and Mims in the front seat, Allen and I in the back, along with two others whom I do not remember. The conversation at lunch had been strained. Mims had made a half-hearted attempt to equate his own kind of scholarship with the New Criticism, which was triumphant by then, but his defense of his own ways faltered when no one answered him. Now he put his arm around Davidson and said, "Don, you know I loved you boys, don't you? I admired your poetry. I did everything I could to help you."

I glanced at Allen. His lips were pressed tightly together and his eyes peered sharply out from under his monumental forehead. I waited for what he would say, but he said nothing.

"You do know that, don't you, Don?" Mims said again.

There was another silence. Then Davidson said drily, "Yes, Dr. Mims. Yes. I know you did."

That was that: the lie went unchallenged out of charity or a desire not to argue or whatever other motive Mr. Davidson may have had. Allen took no exception and our talk engaged another subject. But Allen remembered that day and other days like it. When he was old and sick and worried about the future of Helen and their children, he frequently let his memory dwell on his friends. He often said about Mr. Davidson, "He was too good to Dr. Mims. He never opposed him. He never held him properly accountable for what he did to us."

II

ONE OF THE problems I face in remembering Allen is trying to bridge the gaps and to establish contexts. For example, I saw very little of him when he was married to Isabella and never set eyes on her, though I have heard Allen and others speak of her, and I have read the letters she wrote to Andrew Lytle when Allen was hiding from her in Monteagle and their marriage was breaking up. He taught at Minnesota, with frequent leaves to lecture and teach in India and Italy and France and England and to read his poetry at colleges and universities throughout the United States. He continued to befriend young writers, notably John Berryman whom he brought to Minneapolis. I would see Allen occasionally, at Vanderbilt or elsewhere, and I would have the sense that as life went on and his breath grew shorter and the wrinkles in his face deepened, he stayed essentially the same.

When I first visited him in 1943, he wore a suit that had been made by a Princeton tailor, and I remember thinking what a dapper little man he was. He was one of the few men I have known who could carry a cane without embarrassment, and one night at a party, his dress shirt held together with antique gold studs, he peered through a monocle at Red Warren and declared himself to have been the simplest and most unsophisticated student ever to have attended Vanderbilt. "God damned if I thought so," Red replied. We all laughed, but perhaps at the time neither Red nor I understood Allen's meaning. He was wonderfully polite, and he had such a startlingly good memory that he could recall what you had talked about the last time he had seen you and pick up the conversation as if months had not intervened.

I never felt that I was out of touch with him, and because of this, it seemed to me easy to go backward in time and to imagine the milieus through which he had passed. La Closerie des Lilas is busy and crowded now, and doubtless different in its furnishings and decorations than it was in 1928. But I can fancy Allen and the insomnious Ford Madox Ford sitting at one of the tables, sipping cognac and playing dominoes, or several blocks north, Allen and Hemingway warming themselves over a brazier at an outside table at Les Deux Magots. During that year in Paris, Allen developed his close friendship for John Peale Bishop. Bishop had been born in West Virginia, but Allen thought of him as a southerner, which is, I think, the way Bishop defined himself. In the course of his career, Allen knew almost all of his literary contemporaries: he considered Eliot one of his two mentors. (Ransom was the other.) He expressed affection not only for Ford and Bishop, but for St. John Perse, Malcolm Cowley, Yvor Winters, E. E. Cummings, Archibald MacLeish and many others, and he served on the jury that awarded the Bollingen Prize to Ezra Pound. But Allen's best friends remained the ones he had made in college, though at one time or another, his relationships with most of them were strained.

In 1956, the surviving Fugitives, which was most of them then, gathered in Nashville to hash over the past. Their private sessions, in which their number was increased by a few critics and privileged observers, were slow to get underway. Dorothy Bethurum Loomis set them off in a bad direction by asking why none of them had written an epic. And William Yandell Elliot, who on that night seemed to talk incessantly, was loath to let the matter drop. Still, there they were, all of them changed in the thirty odd years since they had met and read one another's poetry and published their magazine. All of them were also who they were, the successors of who they had been; and together they seemed to me to augment their individual selves.

As I have already remarked, the first of the Fugitives I met was Donald Davidson. He was the first and best writing teacher I ever had, and whatever the subject, his performance in the classroom was extraordinary. It is curious that from the 1940s on, he seldom, if ever, taught contemporary poetry. In addition to his writing classes, he offered courses in the English lyric and in modern British and modern American fiction, in which he included the work of many southerners and most of his friends. At Mr. Davidson's instigation, I first read *Night Rider* and *The Fathers* and *The Long Night* and *The Sound and the Fury*. We read James and Crane and Hemingway too, whom Davidson liked, and Ellen Glasgow, whom he did not like. Occasionally—as with Glasgow or, more notably, T. S. Stribling—he would give comic dissertations at an author's expense, his pale blue eyes glittering with amused malice. But most of the time, he talked about what he admired, making expert thematic interpretations and offering lessons in narrative technique. After I had been teaching at Vanderbilt for a few years, Mr. Davidson gave up the modern fiction courses, and I was greatly intimidated by the notion of following in his footsteps. I taught so badly that I had to be rescued by a student old enough to have been my mother—one of those aging ladies who take a course now and then. She followed me to my office after class one day and said, "You're doing just fine. But you need to stop apologizing for not being Mr. Davidson."

Mr. Davidson. He was a very formal man, and to the best of my knowledge, nobody of my generation ever called him Don. He taught with grace and received questions with equanimity, but he was stern outside the classroom. Knocking on his office door required a measure of courage, and when you were admitted you stated your business and got out the minute it was done. Helen Ransom was so frightened of him that once, when she failed to turn in a paper on time, she blacked her eye with makeup and told him she had been in an accident. Even after I was his colleague at Vanderbilt, though I liked him immensely, I seldom felt totally comfortable with him. He would joke, he would make small talk, but I always felt that there was a line I could not cross, a ritual of demeanor that had to be maintained between youth and experience. He was warmest, it seemed to me, when he was telling about his early days at Vanderbilt or his experiences in France during World War I. For a while, he had served as a billeting officer, and he had gone from door to door looking for housing with a private from Louisiana as his interpreter. When he told this story, he would stand up to demonstrate how French housewives recoiled in shocked astonishment when they heard this Cajun mutilate their language. I was driving him home once, and he admonished me for pulling out into heavy traffic. I told him to have faith and we would be spared. "Faith might get us into the next world," he said, "but it's not going to save us from your foolishness in this one."

He was a learned man, as well educated as anyone I have encountered. Like many of his generation in the South, he had got his Greek and Latin in high school. He had a Masters degree from Vanderbilt—conferred two years after he had joined the Vanderbilt faculty—but like the other major Fugitives, he had for the most part read on his own. He knew English literature from its beginnings, not only the primary works, but much of the scholarship and criticism. His knowledge of politics and history is documented in his books, and he could discourse authoritatively on apples and the history of musical instruments and the plastic arts. He said one of my papers reminded him of what the result might have been if Watteau had done a portrait of the devil.

He was a good poet, and one wonders how much better his work could have been if, like Allen, he had made a full commitment to his poetry. Unlike Allen, he put his family first. He married in the summer of 1918 and went to France a few weeks later; his daughter Mary was born while he was overseas. His Puritan temperament would never have allowed him to keep his wife in poverty or to let someone else care for his child. Instead of living by his wits as Allen did, Davidson taught at a high school, then at Cumberland University, and finally for decades at Vanderbilt University. He edited a book page that was syndicated in several southern papers. His poetry languished while he fulfilled his responsibility to those he loved.

But that, of course, is not the whole story. He was drawn to politics and political engagement. Allen saw *I'll Take My Stand* the way we have come to see it more than half a century later: as a collection of cautionary images warning against the idea that industrial growth and scientific innovation will solve the problems of humankind. Other Agrarians saw their endeavor in other ways, and for a while some of them—notably Ransom—defended it vigorously; but Davidson, alone, both conceived of it as a blueprint for political action and continued to think of it as such for the rest of his life. Between 1938 and 1961, he published no books of verse, and only a handful of his poems appeared in magazines. He wrote a textbook that sold well and that he revised through five editions, but most of his energy was spent in defending the largely Agrarian principles in which he believed.

It seemed to be Mr. Davidson's misfortune that his political adversaries were able to define their conflict with him almost totally in terms of race; but in fact he collaborated in the definition. He told me that when he first came to Vanderbilt, he was friendly with the black professors at Fisk University, met with them socially as well as professionally, but ceased his intercourse with them when the push for racial equality began. In his judgment, the civil rights movement was a vehicle for political upheaval. Even had he not believed this, he would have opposed the movement on its merits, and his stubborn devotion to a platform built on the hypothesis of white supremacy caused both him and his friends a good deal of pain.

From those he considered his friends, he demanded absolute loyalty: you had to agree with him one hundred percent—less would not suffice—and you had to put your agreement into action. Since this was impossible for me, and for most of us, my relationship with him, particularly during times of racial strife, was awkward. He engaged in quixotic efforts to stem the tide of social change by legal action. Mrs. Davidson, herself immensely learned, had earned, among other degrees, an LL.B. She had helped the classical scholar Clyde Pharr translate the Justinian Code into English, and she helped Mr. Davidson develop positions that practicing attorneys who opposed the civil rights movement filed with the courts. Judges rejected these arguments, usually without a hearing, but with each new litigation, Mr. Davidson took new hope. Finally, he had to accept defeat, though he never modified his convictions.

In the last years of his life, he was greatly mellowed. He stopped fighting losing battles, renewed old friendships, some of which had faltered in the fifties, and he became the unofficial custodian of the Fugitive-Agrarian past. He renewed the copyright on *I'll Take My Stand*; he wrote the introduction for the Peter Smith reprint of the *Fugitive*; in his fine poem written for Allen's sixtieth birthday, he evoked memories of a long ago visit to Caroline and Allen at Benfolly, and said in a letter to Allen that the affection expressed in the verses—not only for Allen, but for others who had been there—was meant for the present as well as for the past. By 1960, he would sit with a glass of bourbon in his hand, a radical departure from his abstemiousness of the forties and fifties, and talk of his friends and the work they had written in a spirit and mood that were generous and relaxed.

The Fugitive I knew least well, aside from those whom I knew hardly at all, was John Crowe Ransom. My wife Jane knew him much better. She and Helen Ransom were very close, and Jane had visited the Ransoms in Gambier and had been maid of honor in Helen's wedding to Duane For-

27

man in 1945. One Sunday afternoon in 1948, when Jane and I were visiting her family, one of Jane's aunts, who knew I wanted to meet him and had a talent for taking charge of all situations, telephoned Mr. Ransom, who was a block away at his mother's house, and invited him over. He was short, possibly even shorter than Allen, but he was rounder in face and body; he peered at the world with kind eyes through spectacles and seemed more avuncular than debonair. I was impressed that day and forever after by his courtliness and his gift for language. As shamelessly glad as I was to meet him, I felt guilty that his own afternoon had been interrupted. He had come out of charity and his affection for Jane, but nothing in his manner suggested that he had been inconvenienced. He bowed to Jane's aunt and to her mother. When the ladies were seated, he took a narrow, straight-back chair, in which he managed, by what means I do not know, to sit erect as he must have been taught to do as a child and at the same time to look perfectly comfortable.

He was the center of attention, for me as a hero, for the others as a guest. He talked for an hour, to Jane and me about literature and to the old ladies, as I thought of them then, about mundane affairs, keeping both conversations alive and separate. His voice was higher than Allen's and his diction more southern, but it was absolutely precise, and his speech was marked with linguistic surprises in the same way that his poetry was. I never met another poet who seemed to me so perfectly the person to have written his work as Mr. Ransom. The turns of phrase in his conversation mimicked the patterns of his verse; the juxtapositions of ideas, the vocabulary were common to his informal utterance and to his art. One evening, a decade after Mr. Ransom's death, Donald Davie read some of Mr. Ransom's poems to a small group at a dinner party, and even though Donald reads poetry better than any other person I have ever heard, that night his cadences, his accent seemed to me totally wrong. He was not Mr. Ransom, and I had to adjust my way of listening to reach belatedly the obvious conclusion that Mr. Ransom's work transcends his own tonalities and phrasings. But it remains difficult for me to keep this conclusion in mind.

One night Mr. Davidson and Mr. Ransom were reminiscing about old Vanderbilt days. Kirkland Hall, then the main building on the Vanderbilt campus, burned while Mr. Ransom was an undergraduate. He was at the gymnasium when he got word of the fire; still in his gymnasium costume which, he said, consisted of trousers and a kind of tunic held by a belt around the waist, he went to help. By the time he got to the building most of the furniture had been removed. He saved the chancellor's wastebasket. Then he returned to the building and met Professor McGill who was coming from the chemistry laboratory with a large bottle in his hand. Mr. Ransom asked if he could be of service, and McGill replied that yes, he could. The bottle contained nitroglycerin. "Take it," McGill said, "and put it in a safe place."

"Where did you put it, John?" Mr. Davidson asked.

"I decided to put it under the steps of Kissam Hall," Mr. Ransom replied.

Kissam Hall had been the boys' dormitory. There was a silence while those of us who were listening tried to figure out why Mr. Ransom should have thought of the boys' dormitory as a "safe place." But as he would never have said, he was not thinking of safety. As always, he was seeking the chivalrous course, and who better to put at risk than the boys.

"Did you leave a warning?" Mr. Davidson asked.

"Yes," Mr. Ransom said with the kind of ironic understatement that marks his poetry. "I made an appropriate sign."

Later, when Mr. Ransom joined the Vanderbilt faculty, Dr. Mims's office adjoined the classroom where he taught. For several weeks, Mims made a point of being in his office with the door open when Mr. Ransom's classes met. Finally he said, "Ransom, I'm going to close my door. You're doing well, and I have only one criticism of your teaching. When the bell rings, you dismiss the class. Don't do that. Always keep them overtime so they'll know there's more where that came from."

I think Mr. Ransom did not like Dr. Mims any better than Allen liked him, but he would never have declared his animosity as bluntly as Allen did. He would talk sometimes about the "old way" of teaching literature. "Open your books to page 50," the professor would say. The professor, unnamed by Mr. Ransom but clearly Dr. Mims, would read through the poem, gaze out the window for a silent moment, then say, "Isn't that beautiful? Now turn to page 52."

According to those who studied under him, Mr. Ransom's classroom performance deteriorated after Dr. Mims closed his door. He spent most of his time in class reading aloud, and Lewis Simpson recalls that he read all of *Daisy Miller* in a summer term. But he was generous with his time and with his wisdom when students came to his office, and he never lost the ability to lecture well. At a poetry workshop at Iowa, he spent most of an hour discussing the prosody of "Sing a song of sixpence," scanning lines on the blackboard and pointing out how much could be gained or lost by the changing of a single beat.

This was in the late forties, and he was not popular among many of the Iowa faculty. I think some of them were put off by his good manners, and more of them by his apolitical stance. At a party following his lecture, two or three of the younger Iowa professors asked him if he did not think that his sort of criticism was "inorganic," meaning not "relevant," a word much in vogue in those days. Mr. Ransom smiled and said he thought his method quite organic in the sense that it helped the reader fully to perceive a work of art. He took possession of their term, and even though they attacked him from different angles for the rest of the evening, they never got it back. He was tougher than he appeared and his literary integrity was absolute. As an editor, he rejected work by friends such as Lytle, Warren, and Brooks, and acquaintances such as Mary McCarthy and her husband at the time, Edmund Wilson. He kept no artifacts. He threw away letters as soon as he had answered them, and he made no effort to preserve a manuscript once it was in print.

I met Red Warren when Paul Engle brought him to lunch at our apartment in Iowa City in 1948. What I remember best about that day is that Red had recently learned that he was allergic to tobacco. He had bought some cigarettes named John Alden, which, the package said, spoke for themselves. They were made from dried lettuce and apparently they gave scant satisfaction. Red smoked one after another, and each John Alden seemed to make him more desperate for the real thing. When I saw him a few months later, he had quit smoking altogether, which Allen, in spite of his emphysema, was unable to do until a short time before he died. Red was taller than Allen, more muscular, and decidedly less handsome. Allen enjoyed telling about the first time he saw Red. Walter Clyde Curry of the Vanderbilt English department allowed students to use his typewriter. Allen was typing a poem in Curry's office when Red came in. "He was," Allen said, "the strangest looking boy I had ever seen. He was redheaded and ugly, and he moved in an awkward, shuffling way as if his bones were not properly articulated."

Red said to Allen, "Have you written a poem?"

"Yes."

"I have too," Red said. "Let's exchange poems."

They did, and their friendship began.

Red is a generous man and a good raconteur even though he talks so fast that his words often run together. Stories that he reads and hears seem always to take shape in his mind as images. At the Fugitives' reunion, he closed the formal proceedings by telling of a study done on why girls were sexually active. Some said they had unhappy home lives; some blamed their poverty. Finally, one girl said, "I likes it." That, Red concluded, was what the Rockefeller Foundation was going to find out about why the Fugitives wrote. They "had no alibis." A quarter of a century later at the reunion of the Agrarians, Red was still telling stories: of an old grandmother in a back room encouraging the children, of a black man in a northern city who missed the warmth and friendliness of his native South. In his ordinary conversation, he

31

told stories about almost everything: French immigrants to Kentucky and famous funerals, political campaigns and duels and eating contests, other writers and his own literary experiences, but only rarely did he seem to reveal his most personal thoughts.

In 1977, on a visit to Vanderbilt, Red stayed with Jean and Alex Heard. Jean put a copy of my *Requiem for the Renascence* on his bedside table. Though he had had his own copy of *Requiem* for several months, he read it for the first time that night; the next morning, he called me and we met for lunch. In this book, I had said that the southern literary renascence was largely ended because the southern sense of community had become fragmented and the southern sense of the sacred had been lost. This is what Red wanted to talk about, and as usual, he began with a narrative. Not long before, in Minneapolis, a man who claimed to have been in Vanderbilt when Red was, sent up his card and asked if he might come to Red's room. He was, Red said, "corpulent, expensively dressed and pathetically eroded by hard work and dissipation." He had brought a briefcase full of photographs: a few of his home, a "mansion," some of his house in the country, another estate with a lawn that sloped to water where power boats were tied up at his dock. He had baby pictures of his daughters, but gave these short shrift in his haste to get to photographs of their debuts. Finally, he said, "I'm enormously rich. I have more money than I ever dreamed of. But I'm as lonely as God, and I appreciate your letting me talk to you."

This story was Red's image for the disintegration of community and the confusion of moral values, and the first point he wanted to make was that moral confusion and community fragmentation were not confined to the South. He agreed that the southern renascence was ended, at least in part, for the reasons I had elaborated in *Requiem*, but things were changing everywhere, and we should not look for a repetition of literary movements or ask the questions about life and art that we had asked twenty or even ten years ago. He said that his community was not on Redding Road in

Fairfield, Connecticut, where he and Eleanor hardly knew their neighbors, but in New Haven and San Francisco and Nashville and Paris and London and Rome and all the other places where they had friends.

He spoke of *A Place To Come To* which was soon to appear. He pointed out that he was dedicating it to his brother and sister as if this were a clue about how the novel should be read. Although he did not say so, it was clear that this was the last novel he intended to write. He was almost angry in his insistence that it should be properly understood and not be approached or interpreted as if it were *All the King's Men*. He would make many more trips to the South before he died, but with *A Place*, which is the most significantly autobiographical of his novels, fresh in his mind, he seemed to be comparing his past to his present and even wondering what course his life might have taken if, like Tate and Davidson and Lytle, he had stayed in or returned to the South, or like Ransom, settled for life in a town like Gambier. By this time, Allen had been in Tennessee for several years, and he often said of Red, "He is living in the wrong place and seeing the wrong people."

That he might indeed be living in the wrong place seemed to have crossed Red's mind more than once. Usually he was reluctant to talk about the Agrarians and understandably so. He had been obliged again and again publicly to recant and apologize for his essay on race in *I'll Take My Stand*. But when I suggested that small family farms were no longer economically feasible, he disagreed profoundly and said that in essence the Agrarians had been right: not in the details, but in the principles that underlay them. He was defending the culture into which he had been born and he seemed briefly to be wondering if he should have broken with it as completely as he had. The moment of doubt, if doubt it was, passed quickly. He had made his choices and he seemed content with them.

Andrew Lytle was the only one of the Agrarians who attempted to put their theory into practice. Allen's brother

Ben gave him and Caroline a farm in Kentucky where, according to report, they had house guests much of the time and took down the draperies to make costumes for charades and sat by the fire or on the porch, drinking and discussing literature. But Allen did not pretend to be a farmer. A man who worked at Benfolly, with little if any direction from Allen, said, "Now, Mr. Tate. He ain't much of a hand with a hoe." Andrew knew how to chop, and he continued to raise a garden until he was past eighty. He spent the best days of his youth at Cornsilk, his father's farm in Alabama. He began *The Long Night* sitting on a stump in the Cornsilk woods, and he never forgave the Tennessee Valley Authority for creating a lake which covered the property.

I first met Andrew in Iowa City where he had come to teach for a year, and where he and Jane and I felt alien. We were not accustomed to a climate where snow fell early and lingered on the ground and where for weeks at a time the temperature would remain below zero. In 1947, the town and the campus were crowded with veterans. Housing was scarce; businesses had more trade than they could handle. The rudeness of landlords and merchants infected the general population. When Andrew and Edna arrived in Iowa City with two children, the university offered them an apartment in a converted Quonset hut that had been flooded the spring before. There were stains on the walls and mud on the floor; the furniture was warped and soggy. Later, they occupied Paul Engle's house while he was on leave and Andrew was acting director of the Writers' Workshop.

After the Lytles moved, Paul discovered that one of his storm windows was broken and he asked Andrew if he knew how the breakage had happened. I have often wondered what Paul meant by this question. I knew him well during my Iowa years and liked him then and later, but I have never fully understood him. The culture in which he had grown up, his manners, his way of getting through the world were different from mine and certainly different from Andrew's. Paul said what he meant to the point of bluntness and, paradoxical as this may seem in a poet, worried little about subtleties and implications that to Andrew were often more important than the actual utterance. I do not think Paul meant to accuse Andrew of duplicity, but Andrew felt himself being accused—of having broken the window and left without mentioning it in the hope of not having to pay for the damage. He never fully forgave Paul, just as later, he never fully forgave Helen Tate for standing in the doorway of her house in Sewanee and not inviting him in one afternoon when he had come to see Allen.

Andrew's sense of honor is unbending, but it has another dimension. In 1952, Jane and I were in Gainesville, and I accompanied Andrew to one of his classes. He taught well, but without his usual flair. He was silent during our drive back to his house. When he had parked and stopped the engine, he did not get out of the car. What was on his mind was an old debt.

He told me that years before, when he had needed money, a friend named George Haight, a Hollywood producer, had given him five thousand dollars. "Consider it a loan." Haight had said. "I don't need it now. If I ever do, I'll let you know."

Now Haight had fallen on hard times, and he had written to Andrew. Andrew had just built a house in Gainesville. His daughters were in school. He could live on his salary, but he did not have five thousand dollars or enough room in his budget to borrow it and pay it back.

"What are you doing to do?" I asked.

"Pay him," Andrew said without hesitation.

"Maybe you could send part of it now and more later."

"No," he replied, "I must send it all. I'll sell the farm."

Andrew's farm was near Portland, Tennessee. He and Edna had gone there after they left Iowa, and for a year or so, he had tried to farm and write. This had not worked, so he had taken the job at Florida, but he had kept the farm as a place to go back to. When he had been there, he had overseen the cultivation of the land. He had patched and painted the house, had a well dug, and laid a brick terrace in the angle where the wings joined. He had gathered mushrooms from his own woods—sometimes to the consternation of his visitors. He loved his farm and had hoped to spend many happy years there. Now he was forced to give it up to fulfill an old and undocumented obligation.

III

ALLEN FIRST saw Helen Heinz in Minneapolis in 1964 when she enrolled in his class in modern poetry. He was still married to Isabella Gardner; Helen was a nun in habit. He was careful to explain later that she was already in the process of leaving her order and that his marriage, for him at least, had begun to pall. But neither of them knew anything about the other when, as he told it, their eyes met and they began to fall in love. "More and more," Allen said, "my remarks were directed to her until it was as if she were the only other person in the room." After one of his Crane lectures, she joined the throng at the door waiting to congratulate him. "When I touched her hand," he said, "and looked at the white flesh of her wrist, I knew I was going to marry her."

The romantic quality of this beginning was ironically enhanced by the difference in their ages and by their shared religion. He was sixty-five; she was thirty-one. He had taken himself out of communion with the church when he married Isabella, but never once in his life did he cease to believe in the Catholic God and in everything this belief implied: good and evil; virtue and vice; death and judgment. To live on the edge was part of Allen's temperament and character. The same psychological need that inspired him to enter into combat with his enemies and fall out with his friends was manifested most intensely in his relationship with the church. He believed in God's mercy, but he also believed in hell, and he believed the church when it told him that his love affairs and his irregular marriages put his soul in jeopardy. In his case, the trick was not to die without sufficient warning, to reserve time at the end of his life for a conversion of will and an act of contrition. This would involve straightening out his physical life too, restraining the appetites that he had compulsively indulged for almost half a century. Marrying a woman younger than his daughter, too young to have been the mother of his oldest grandchild, dimmed the prospects of such a reformation. But he was in love, death seemed remote, and as always, he was willing to risk everything.

Allen said that Helen had been mistreated in the convent, and her unhappiness there may have put her in a rebellious mood. In any case, she was in love too, perhaps for the first time in her life. Allen attempted to date her while she was still wearing her veil. She put him off, but she came alone to his house to discuss one of her papers, and as soon as she was discharged from her order, they began to go out together. Allen talked to her about marriage before June when Isabella took him to Spoleto in an effort to save their marriage. Allen and Helen continued their relationship with letters, some of which Isabella intercepted, and in the fall, Allen came back to the United States and stayed at Monteagle for the rest of the year. He was editing a special issue of the *Sewanee Review*, to memorialize T. S. Eliot, but most weekends, he would meet Helen in Nashville. He divorced Isabella in January, and in July he and Helen were married in the city hall at Murfreesboro, Tennessee. They lived in Monteagle and Nashville until September, went to Greensboro for the fall term, and returned to Vanderbilt for the spring semester.

Helen apparently had no idea of Allen's amorous past. She knew of his marriages, of course, but he could explain those away. He doubtless told Helen, as he told everybody else, that the Meriwethers—Caroline's mother's family—were all paranoid and could be communicated with "only in that medium." Isabella's life and personality and family were bizarre enough for Allen to make a case against her also, and Helen was a willing believer. She was ignorant too of the literary world except for the fact that she had married a famous writer. Allen often said that he had never heard her say anything brilliant, but he had never heard her say anything stupid either. She met many of his literary friends: the Cheneys, of course, and Andrew, the Warrens, the Cowleys, Walker Percy, Eudora Welty, and others. She was familiar with the names of Pound and Eliot and Ransom, and she soon appeared to be easy among literary people.

She discovered the vanity of poets, and she teased Allen. Once when they were having lunch with Jane and me, our daughter Pam came in from school carrying her American literature text book. Allen asked to see "whom she was studying," but, as Helen knew, he really wanted to see if any of his work were included, and none was.

"Well," Helen said, smiling and looking at him with eyes that were filled with affection, "you're not as famous as you thought you were, are you?"

"I guess I'm not," Allen replied.

We all laughed, including Pam who, like most women of whatever age, found Allen charming.

The first summer of Allen and Helen's marriage they were attentive to each other and conscious of each other, even when they were apart. At parties they would separate for brief periods, but they seemed always to be drifting back toward each other or glancing at each other when they had to be apart. Allen spoke often of her when she was not present, and she spoke of him. She told Jane that she knew she and Allen would not have many years together, but they meant to make the most of what they had. She planned to accompany him when he went to read or lecture: she wanted to be with him and to meet more of his friends and to share his fame. They intended to spend the summer after their wedding in Italy where Allen knew the landmarks and spoke the language. Helen said that however short their time might be, she was happy now in every dimension, every aspect of her marriage. He loved her too and made no secret of it. One day when Jane called to speak to Helen, she could hear Allen's voice after he had put down the phone. "Darling, darling," he said, his tone joyful and affectionate. "Jane wants to speak to you, darling."

Then, before the honeymoon was properly ended, Helen got pregnant. They were astonished and not particularly happy. They were building a house in Sewanee to which they intended to retire; now with construction well under way, a nursery had to be added. In May, 1967, when Allen's stint at Vanderbilt was over, they moved to Monteagle and lived next door to Andrew where Allen had stayed when he was separating from Isabella. They assumed the baby would be born after they returned to Minneapolis for Allen's last year there, but at the end of August, when Helen came for what she thought would be a routine visit to her Nashville obstetrician, she went into labor. She wanted to telephone Allen whom she had dropped off at the Cheneys' in Smyrna, but she was dilating so rapidly that her doctor made her wait to call until she was checked into the hospital and prepared for delivery. When she did reach Allen, she told him not only that the baby was coming prematurely, but that there would be not one baby, but two. Only then did she learn that she would have twins.

By the time Helen called Smyrna, Allen and Fannie and Lon were comfortably settled into the cocktail hour. Even without hearing Allen's voice, Helen would have known this to be the case, and Smyrna was twenty-five miles from Nashville. She called Mary Dudley Fletcher, whose husband Frank, a Nashville businessman, had been an undergraduate at Vanderbilt with Allen. The Fletchers were at the hospital when Allen and Fannie arrived. They stayed to comfort Allen while Helen endured a difficult delivery. The babies were rushed, as soon as they were born, into the neonatal intensive care unit. They were both in perilous health and the younger one was very sick indeed, but Allen did not at first realize this. He asked when the babies were going to be brought to Helen to nurse. Getting no satisfactory answer, he let the matter drop and went with Mary Dudley and Frank to spend the night at their house.

Jane and I were out of town when the twins were born on Thursday. We got home on Sunday night, and the next morning, Allen telephoned. "Jane," he said, "I have a little boy." He paused, but before Jane could congratulate him, he said, "And Jane, I have another little boy." Helen had left the hospital, and that afternoon Jane and I went to visit her and Allen at the Fletchers' house. Helen was pale and sore and exhausted. Being a nurse, she knew the danger her children were in; but Allen, who knew less about medical matters than she knew about literature, had no inkling that anything was wrong. On the night the twins were born, Mary Dudley had found some toilet articles for Allen to use, but he had had to sleep in Frank's pajamas, and he wore some of Frank's clothes the next day. He had his own clothes now, but he was still drinking Frank's whisky which, according to Mary Dudley, he had been doing with zeal since the babies had arrived.

Another couple was present that afternoon, a man ten years older than Allen who was said to be an ardent womanizer and a lady about Allen's age who was said to be the man's latest conquest. Allen seemed to admire the old man's energy, but given Helen's youth and his recent paternity, he felt superior. At the hospital, he had said to a technician, "I'm exactly twice as old as my wife." The technician had replied, "Well, you're doing all right, ain't you?" Allen was euphoric during our visit. When we left, he told Mary Dudley that he had been holding up under the strain since the birth of the babies. Now that the worst appeared to be over, he was going to get drunk, which he did. The next morning, Mary Dudley asked him whether he realized that premature babies often failed to survive. "My God!" Allen said. "No. I didn't know that."

His euphoria changed to gloom which was compounded by the recurrence of an old digestive ailment brought on by his week of heavy smoking and drinking. Helen was not feeling well either, but they decided to leave the Fletchers'

41

1956 Fugitive Reunion (left to right: Allen Tate, Merrill
Moore, Robert Penn Warren, John Crowe Ransom,
Donald Davidson).

*Photo by Joe Rudis. Courtesy Photographic Archives,
Vanderbilt University.*

Caroline Gordon and Allen Tate, after their
second marriage, circa 1950.

*Photo by Ralph Morrisey. Courtesy Photographic Archives,
Vanderbilt University.*

Left to right: William Ralston, Allen Tate,
Andrew Lytle, early 1960s.
Courtesy Coulson's Studio (Cowan, Tennessee) and
the University of the South.

Mildred Haun, Tate's editorial assistant
at *Sewanee Review*, ca. 1969.
Courtesy Photographic Archives, Vanderbilt University.

Tate with his sons John and Ben, in Sewanee,
Tennessee, 1970 or 1971.
*Photo by Gale Link. Courtesy Photographic Archives,
Vanderbilt University.*

Allen Tate and Walter Sullivan, December 27, 1971.
Courtesy Pam Chenery.

Tate's seventy-fifth birthday celebration, 1974, in Sewanee,
Tennessee. Clockwise from bottom: Louis D. Rubin, Jr.,
Eudora Welty, Harry Duncan, Cleanth Brooks, Lewis Simpson,
Francis Ferguson, Morton Weisman, Allen Tate, William Jay
Smith, Joseph Frank, Howard Nemerov.
Courtesy Photographic Archives, Vanderbilt University.

Helen Tate, circa 1969.
Courtesy Coulson's Studio, Cowan, Tennessee.

At Aquinas Junior College, Nashville, 1976, on the
occasion of Tate's being presented a gold medal and
certificate for his literary achievement.
Seated: Allen Tate and Ellen Wills
Standing: Frances Cheney, Brainerd Cheney, Jesse Wills

Courtesy Aquinas Junior College, Nashville, Tennessee.

On the same occasion, at Aquinas Junior College.
Seated, left to right: Allen Tate and Walter Sullivan
Standing, left to right: Pringle Patrick,
James Patrick, Jane Sullivan

On the same occasion, at Aquinas Junior College.
Left to right: Helen Tate, Sister Domenica Gobel,
Allen Tate, Marie Aden, John M. Aden, Shailah Jones,
Sister Mary Anthony Barr, John Pritchett, Madison Jones

and return to Monteagle. Jane offered to help them pack, but she thought they were not yet able to take care of themselves, and she asked Mildred Stahlman to help her persuade them to stay with the Cheneys. Mildred headed the neonatal unit at Vanderbilt Hospital. She talked to Helen and Allen and explained to them, as she had earlier, that it might be impossible to save Michael. When Helen's obstetrician also advised against the trip to Monteagle, Helen and Allen agreed to go to Smyrna. A day or two later, it seemed certain that Michael would die. Allen asked me to drive him to Sewanee to consult with the bankers who were financing his house and to arrange for the purchase of a cemetery lot where Michael might be buried.

That day in September, Allen was fretful as we drove up the mountain. Neither Lon, who accompanied us, nor I could find a way to comfort him. The weather was still warm, but the day was overcast and rain fell intermittently. Allen could not decide whether he wanted the car airconditioned. He would say yes and then no. It seemed that every time he opened a window, the rain would start again, and when he closed the window the air grew heavy from the smoke of his cigarettes. He felt bad physically, and he was grieving for Michael. His usual flow of conversation was diminished. But at times like this he demonstrated strength that, on happier occasions, was disguised by his waspishness. His courtesy never faltered. As he fussed over the airconditioning and the window, he asked Lon and me what would make us most comfortable. He said how grateful he was to Mildred Stahlman for the heroic efforts she was making to save his sons and to Mary Dudley and Frank for having sheltered him and Helen. His pain was apparent in his words and in his silences, but his voice was steady.

We met William Ralston and Andrew for lunch at the Holiday Inn at Monteagle. Knowing we would be in a dry county, Lon, a wise veteran of Prohibition days, had brought a flask that we passed around under the table. After a couple of drinks, Allen was able to ask about the plot at the cemetery. Andrew told him that the purchase had been arranged and described the location. Andrew asked him if he wanted to go see it, calling him Brother, which was the way the Fugitives and the Agrarians had addressed each other. Allen said he did not: he knew where it was from Andrew's description. After lunch, I drove to the bank in Sewanee and waited while Allen and Lon went in and came out almost immediately, the business here having taken no more time, and, I suspected, having no more required Allen's presence than the matter of the cemetery. We went back to Monteagle to Andrew's house on the Assembly Grounds, where at this season almost all the other cottages stood empty.

We sat for a while, drinking, in Andrew's study. Bill Ralston had recently given Andrew some stereo equipment and somebody, probably Bill, put on a record. The overture to *Madam Butterfly* came blasting out of the speakers. I think Bill's intention was to make conversation unnecessary, but Allen would not have it. He said, "Turn down the music, Brother, so we can talk." Andrew did, but then he had to do most of the talking. He spoke of work he was having done on his house and of the writing schedule he kept, getting up early enough to be at his desk by five and being finished by eight or nine in the morning. The rest of us spoke inanely about our own schedules until Allen decided that it was time to return to Smyrna. It was not late, perhaps three thirty; but while we had been inside, the clouds had continued to thicken and rain was falling steadily as we drove out of the Assembly Grounds. Allen stared out the window as if he were studying the silent, shuttered houses.

That morning, Fannie had invited me to stay for dinner, and I did. First there were more drinks, and when we got to the table, Lon began to talk about Teilhard de Chardin. Lon had come into the Catholic church—had perhaps been brought there by Caroline's prayers—with a willing heart, but an uneasy mind. His background was literary and political. He had begun as a newspaper reporter, spent many years in Washington as administrative assistant to a senator, and he had written several novels. But he was drawn to science. He read books about scientific theories,

50

and he longed to reconcile the mysteries of his faith with what he considered to be demonstrable scientific truths. He thought Teilhard had made such a reconciliation, and whenever he had the opportunity, he talked endlessly about convergence and the Omega point.

Allen had little patience with Teilhard or with Lon's version of his work, but through most of dinner, he endured Lon's monologue. Then he declared Teilhard's whole system to be nonsense and told Lon to "shut up about Chardin." As we left the table and Lon and Allen and I went into the living room, Lon shifted his focus to the Ascension. He said that Christ could have risen from the earth and ascended toward heaven only in the Ptolemaic system that Copernicus had discredited. It was absurd, he said, to think of heaven being above, since the center of our solar system was the sun. Thanks to the dinner wine, we were far enough into our cups to argue vociferously over this proposition. At last, Allen said, "Lon, I know more about almost everything than you do." For a moment, Lon was silent. Then he said, "Yes, Brother, I know you do." Fannie had been sitting in the darkened dining room saying her rosary. Now she came into the living room and told me to go home and ordered Lon to bed. When I left, Allen was still in his chair, a drink near at hand, a cigarette between his fingers.

Michael survived, and in the fall he was able to leave the hospital. Helen flew down from Minneapolis to get him — John had already been released — and returned to settle in for the Minnesota winter with her family. This, I think, was the best part of her and Allen's life together. She had not planned to have children, but now that she had them she was enormously pleased. Her letters to Jane were filled with news of how the boys were growing and of what they were learning. She sent snapshots of them. Allen was behaving decorously, being charming and thoughtful and absolutely faithful. When he was in the right mood, as he was now, he could take a humorous view of life's aggravations. He had bought a new car and had it fitted with a device that started

51

it every hour to warm the engine. At three o'clock one morning, the car not only started, but caught fire and burned in the Tates' driveway. Allen saw this as the revenge of technology against his Agrarianism and bought a new automobile.

The previous spring in Nashville, he and Helen had rented a house from Lee Jessup, Lon Cheney's sister. The woman who ordinarily did housework for Lee worked for them, and she promised Helen that she would help her when she and Allen came back to Sewanee, but Helen had got her address wrong and could not find her. Helen could not ask Lee where the woman lived, because she and Lee had fallen out over a bedspread that Lee said Helen had ruined and that Helen said was worth a lot less than Lee made her pay for it. So Helen asked Jane to look for the woman and after a good deal of searching Jane found her. This was a small thing, remarkable only for the amount of correspondence it generated. Throughout this time, Helen seemed to be more under Allen's influence than she would ever be again. She could look at the heroic search for a cleaning woman with his sort of irony.

She and Allen came back to Sewanee in June, made a trip to Italy, though shorter than the one they had planned for the summer before, both of them still lively and contented. Helen wrote from Florence that the sky, even in London, had been clear every day of their journey. They would hate to leave Italy, she said, but they missed the children. Then, soon after their return in the middle of July, they lost Michael. They went to Andrew's for dinner as they often did, but this time, for reasons that he could not fathom, Andrew did not want them to come. His feeling of discontent was so strong that he could not bring himself to start cooking. The roast he intended to serve had not been put in the oven when they arrived, and even with his guests in the house, Andrew procrastinated. Then Eleanor Harrison, who lived next door to the Tates, called to say that Michael had been hurt.

The story of what happened that night was pieced together later from what the woman who was sitting with the children said and from what Eleanor saw. The sitter had put Michael in the playpen while she bathed John, but contrary to Helen's instructions, she had not placed the playpen where she could see it. She heard Michael cry. She waited for him to cry again. When he did not, she assumed that nothing was wrong and finished bathing John. Michael had been playing with a plastic toy shaped like a telephone. He had fallen forward with the toy in his mouth and it had been driven into his throat and lodged there. When she found him, the sitter picked Michael up, removed the toy from his mouth, laid him on the bed on his back, and while he choked on blood and vomit, the sitter ran to get Eleanor.

Eleanor had neither children nor medical knowledge, but she did what she knew to do: she called an ambulance, a pediatrician and the Tates. The ambulance came first and took the baby to the hospital. The doctor came to the house, found that Michael had already left, and followed the ambulance. Helen and Allen went directly to the hospital, but the hospital personnel would not allow Helen to go into the emergency room where Michael was being treated. Helen told Jane later that she knew what things needed to be done for Michael and she wanted to be near him to see that they were being done, but she had to wait in the hospital corridor, spending, she later said, the most difficult moments of her life. Then the doctor came with his grim announcement. Given the length of time that Michael had lain on his back while the sitter went for Eleanor and while she and Eleanor waited for the ambulance, Michael was probably dead before he got to the hospital. But exactly when he died was never established.

I was away from Nashville conducting a writers' conference, but Jane went to the funeral. So did the Cheneys and the Fletchers and Ellen and Jesse Wills. Jesse had been one of the Fugitives and, like Frank Fletcher, Allen's lifelong friend. Andrew was there as were a few others, but the group was small, and at the chapel, they sat in a semicircle around the altar and the open casket. Although they were out of communion with the church, Allen and Helen had frequently attended Mass, and a Catholic priest assisted Bill Ralston at Michael's funeral. Jane did not follow the liturgy. Her mind focused on the still, pale face of Michael, and on those of his parents, fully as pale and almost as still as his. Neither of them wept, even when the casket was closed and they began the short trip to the cemetery. Here there were more prayers. The casket was lowered, and Helen and Allen waited, still composed and silent until the grave was filled. Then Helen turned and seemed about to fall until Bill Ralston caught her. All the tears she had held back came now and she clung to Bill with her face against his shoulder.

Jane and I visited Helen and Allen a few days after the funeral. "Helen is very strong," Allen said. She was determined to maintain her ordinary household routines and to face reality. She insisted that we go look at the nursery, which was obviously an afterthought, a room tacked on to their otherwise well designed house. The two cribs were still there and above them two identical crosses fashioned out of nails. The second bed was a reminder of Michael's absence, but his loss was no more acutely felt here than in the rest of the house. Grief had descended on Helen and Allen like a great weariness. It showed in the flatness of their eyes, the deliberation of their speech and movement. Their attention remained on John, where he was, what he was doing, what might threaten his safety.

Five years earlier, in May of 1963, Allen had come from Minneapolis to Sewanee to attend Edna Lytle's funeral. Edna had had cancer of the lung, and she had fought against death in order to be with her daughters and to give them as much of herself as she could. When she knew she could not live, she refused to return to the hospital and she died at home in Andrew's arms. At her burial, in the same cemetery where Michael would be buried in 1968, Allen had stood beside Andrew and cried while Andrew kept his composure. But like Helen and Allen now, Andrew had been heartbroken then. Months after Edna's funeral, thinking Andrew's mourning went on too long, Allen had picked up a line from his own poetry and told Andrew that he should not try "to

54

set up the grave in the house." I thought of this line as we looked at Michael's crib. Later, Andrew remembered too and repeated to Allen what Allen had said to him after the death of Edna.

Whatever else contributed to the enmity that soon developed between Andrew and Allen, the loss of Michael played a major part. "They never forgave me for their being at my house when Michael died," Andrew said. He was never comfortable with the knowledge that they had been there either. On that day, he had felt what he had felt: his premonition was lodged in his memory and it made him uncomfortable. But for Helen and Allen, the death of Michael changed everything.

IV

HELEN SOON got pregnant as Fannie Cheney had predicted she would. "She wants another child to replace Michael," Fannie said, but even as she was bringing another baby into the world, Helen began to worry about money and the future. Suddenly she seemed to realize that Allen was approaching seventy and would probably be dead in ten years—which he was—leaving her with two children. For the present, they were secure. Their house was paid for. Allen was selling his papers to Princeton, and though his invitations were fewer than they once had been, he still gave readings and lectures and he commanded good fees. He had a pension from Minnesota and an annuity from his brother Ben's estate, but these would stop with his death, and that was the problem.

Helen told Jane that she would not go back to work until she had to, but every year she fell further behind in her profession. She did not want to return to work, but neither did she appear to want to scrimp now to save for the future. She remodeled their house, turning the garage into a dining room and adding another garage. She had a swimming pool built. She bought a horse and boarded it in a nearby stable. At the same time, she pressed on Allen the necessity for making more money. She knew that Red Warren had got rich by writing, and she thought that because Allen was almost as famous as Red, his poetry and criticism ought to make him rich too. When Allen convinced her that there was not much profit in poems and essays, she urged him to write whatever would sell, believing, as nonliterary people often do, that a talent to write at all was a talent to write anything.

Allen seemed to be thinking more often than ever of his age and his impending mortality. Until he married Helen, he had always been able to get himself out of what he had got himself into. When he fell in love with Isabella, he divorced Caroline, the knowledge that he was cutting himself off from the church notwithstanding. When he wanted to marry Helen, he left Isabella in Italy and hid out happily at Monteagle with Andrew to protect him. Now he began to realize that his running days were over. His emphysema and his stomach ulcer were getting worse, his energy was failing, and he was becoming increasingly dependent on Helen. He was where he was going to be, in the circumstances he was going to be in for the rest of his life unless Helen decided to change them. Her concerns became his concerns. He echoed her conversation, or rather, translated it into his own superior idiom.

He did what he could to increase his income. He read manuscripts and wrote book reviews. He wrote letters to his distinguished friends and acquaintances, eliciting responses that he could sell to Princeton. He looked for publishers to bring out new editions of his existing work, and when none of these efforts produced adequate results, he made a public issue out of his need for money. Shamelessly he urged his friends to help him get grants and prizes. They did, and he received the $10,000 Ingram Merrill Foundation Award in 1975; the $5,000 Mark Rothko Award, the $5,000 Oscar Williams Award, and the $10,000 National Medal for Literature, all in 1976. He was grateful, but like the woman in the D. H. Lawrence story, he was not satisfied. In 1977, when he was bedridden but as efficiently manipulative as ever, he induced Lon Cheney to try to help him get the Nobel Prize in literature.

Lon appointed a committee of himself, David McDowell and me, and we met at lunch to plan our strategy—or rather to discuss how we would implement the strategy that Allen had planned for us. The discrepancy between the prestige of the prize and the ordinariness of the committee was ironic. All Lon's distinction as a novelist was in the distant past. Mine had never existed. David had been at Kenyon with Cal Lowell and Peter Taylor and Robie Macaulay. He had worked at Random House and briefly had been a partner in McDowell, Obolensky. He had been fired recently by Crown from the last job he would ever have. He claimed to be writing a biography of James Agee, but mostly he was drinking.

Our committee began its deliberations with a drink. Then we had another, and Lon produced a letter he had written for us to send out and Allen's membership roster of the American Academy of Arts and Letters to whom we would send it. The letter rehearsed, though in scant detail, Allen's literary accomplishments and urged the recipients to send endorsements of Allen's nomination to the Nobel committee. David suggested some changes in Lon's prose.

"God damn it!" Lon said, "I've told them to nominate Allen. It's all right like it is."

David sipped his vodka and waited. Then he said, "Lon, you asked us to come here to discuss your letter. If you're not going to let us discuss it, why did you make us come here?"

"Well, all right," Lon replied.

I was content to let him and David negotiate the matter. They took out their pencils and put their heads together. When they were satisfied with the letter, Lon read through the Academy roster to determine which of the members one of us knew personally and therefore could address by his or her first name. Lon and David undertook this procedure with great seriousness.

"Well, I used to know him a long time ago," David said, "I don't know whether he would remember me."

"Maybe, we'd better not use his first name, then," Lon replied. We got to the end of the list. Lon promised to have the letters typed with appropriate salutations. A week later, we signed the letters and mailed them to Allen's friends and to those of his enemies who were in the Academy.

While Allen waited for his prize, he kept busy. Before Helen brought him to Nashville in June, 1975, principally to get him closer to his doctors, Lon had helped lead him back into the church. I had learned that the church had no objection to his and Helen's staying married as long as they lived celibately. Given Allen's deteriorating health, this seemed what they were fated to do in any event. I suggested that Lon speak to Allen, and one day at lunch at the Sewanee Inn, Lon broached the subject. "Well," Allen said, "it might be all right for me, but Helen is a young woman and I don't want to deprive her." We found out later that Helen had already deprived herself, having told Allen that she could no longer bear to listen to his wheezing and panting.

When they left Sewanee in 1976, they were back in full communion, and Allen made the most of their restoration. Helen had bought a house near St. Henry's Church. The priests there called on Allen and brought him the sacraments. He told them he needed secretarial help and they sent it. Volunteers among his fellow parishioners came to take his dictation, type and mail his letters, and organize the responses for sale to Princeton. Between stints of letter-writing and entertaining visitors, he tried to think of still more ways to get money. He wrote his nephew, Ben's son, asking that Ben's will be changed to have his annuity from Ben's estate continue to be paid, after his death, to Helen. Ben had written his will when Allen was married to Isabella. By the time Allen married Helen, Ben was in a nursing home, his mind damaged. "If he had known about Helen, he would have provided for her," Allen said, which, given Ben's generosity to Allen, may have been true. But Ben's son remained adamant—Allen blamed his wife—in spite of Allen's many letters and telephone calls.

Brooding over how his sons would be educated, Allen enlisted Lon's aid once more. Lon and Fannie donated a thousand dollars to a fund for the education of the Tate boys and invited Allen's friends to make similar contributions. Some did, but the take fell short of Allen's expectations. Continuing to ponder the problem of what he conceived to be his poverty, Allen decided that Vanderbilt owed him something. "Every time I've been introduced on a platform," he said, "here or in England or on the continent, the introduction has referred to my education at Vanderbilt." He totaled up the number of times he had been introduced, assigned a value to them, and told Alex Heard, then chancellor of the university, that Vanderbilt owed him $35,000. Alex agreed that the figure was reasonable, but said he had no budget out of which to make payment. Though he seldom left his bed, Allen asked Alex to furnish him a car and driver at university expense on the ground that Allen was a distinguished alumnus. Again Alex claimed to see justice in the request, but had no funds with which to grant it.

Finally, in a display of effrontery that seemed extreme even for Allen, he asked Caroline for money. At the time of their divorce, she and Allen owned a house in Princeton. According to Allen, Ben Tate had furnished the down payment, but Caroline had used her own money to make repairs and to add an ell. This was true, but it did not accurately describe the situation. Ben had given them money for the first house they bought in Princeton, and Caroline had paid for the addition. But this house, Benbrackets, was sold; the Tates bought a second house in Princeton, sold that, and then bought a third, which, once more, Caroline remodeled. Ben's money was still in the equation, but Allen's interest in the third house was not as clear as he conceived it to be. He spoke as if they had owned only one house. He said that after their separation, Caroline called him and suggested that they sign the house over to their granddaughter Caroline Wood, who, Caroline Gordon told Allen, had developed epilepsy and needed to be provided for. Allen agreed, but he said he had been tricked. Nancy had the house put in her name—to prevent, Allen said, some ne'erdowell's marrying young Caroline for her money. Now, according to Allen,

Caroline Gordon had got the house back, had sold it, and Allen wanted his share.

For Caroline, her final separation from Allen had been devastating. In the fall of 1956, Allen had left her and gone to India, betraying the affection that she had retained for him in spite of his many previous infidelities. Her second marriage to him had indeed demonstrated the triumph of hope over experience, but her hope had been strong. Now she found herself alone, with little money—Allen had all but emptied their bank account—and no immediate means of making a living. She had expected to spend the fall with Allen in Minneapolis. Instead she remained in Princeton, got a job teaching in New York, and began to build a new life for herself. She suspected that this time her separation from Allen was permanent, but she had no intention of giving him a divorce. She had come into the Catholic church determined to live by its rules. She saw by now that Allen's fervor had not been equal to hers, but she believed that it ought to have been, and she did not propose to breach the sacrament of marriage. Finally, her confessor told her to divorce him, not for his sake, but for hers. She could not prevent his adulteries by making him stay married, and for her own peace, she needed to get him out of her life. Now, almost twenty years after their divorce was final, Allen asked her to share the money she had got for their house. She said no. Then engaging her novelist's sense of irony, she offered him her part of any future royalties on *The House of Fiction*—an anthology they had jointly edited in 1951.

Bitter as she was over his treatment of her, Caroline retained great affection for Allen as he did for her, and she would have pitied him had she seen him. He spent the last years of his life in a room barely large enough to accommodate a single bed, a small nightstand, a small chest, and two straight chairs. For a while, he had a telephone, which he used most frequently when Helen was out. Once he called Caroline and said that he still loved her, but he hung up when he heard Helen's footsteps in the hall. Not long afterwards, Helen had his phone removed. He had a table radio and inscribed photographs of Eliot and Ransom—"My two teachers," he called them—on his wall. Even this much furniture crowded the room, and when Jane and I went together to see him, we had to seat ourselves carefully, one of us beside the bed, the other beyond it against the wall. Then an oxygen tank was added, and there was hardly any space in the room to move at all.

Allen had not taken care of himself. In January, 1970, about a month after Benjamin was born, he came from Sewanee to Vanderbilt Hospital to be circumcised. Given his reputation and the fact that at seventy he was a new father, he was understandably sensitive about the surgery, but his physicians were more concerned about his lungs. His capacity to breathe was greatly reduced by emphysema. He was told to stop smoking, to buy and ride an exercycle, and to do breathing exercises. He bought the exercycle, but it stood unused in his study. Briefly he tried to reduce his smoking, but soon he was smoking as much as ever; and the other exercises, he did once or twice if at all. Swimming would have been good for him, but he declined to be seen in a bathing suit. He quoted an elderly lady of his acquaintance: "I don't want to expose a shriveled apple."

With his health failing and Helen arguing more and more vigorously the case of her insecure future, Allen developed a dual personality. Like Dickens' Mr. Wemmick, he had one set of sentiments for use at home and another for the rare occasions when he went alone in public. He had come to Nashville on the bus for his circumcision. I had met him at the station and taken him to the hospital; when he was released, Jane and I checked him out and took him to lunch at the University Club. He had a bloody mary and a cigarette, wondered if his bladder would betray him during the trip home if he had another drink, and decided to risk it. I had visited him every day he was in the hospital, but often when I was there some of his friends from his college years were also present and with typical good manners, Allen directed the conversation to their interests and concerns.

Now, he wanted to talk about literature and literary people: as we did, some of the paleness left his face, and he seemed, in spite of the cigarettes he was lighting, to breathe more easily. At the bus station, depression appeared to overtake him. Perhaps he was tired or the vodka that had stimulated him earlier was making him sleepy. For whatever reason, his liveliness died as he boarded the bus to go back to Sewanee.

He was gloomy at home and caught up in Helen's desire for money, but to see his life only in these terms is to oversimplify it. He was a burden to Helen, and sometimes his friends were a burden to her, which is one of the reasons she fell out with Andrew. Allen loved John and Benjamin, and he was patient with them, but he was incapable of doing anything to help care for them. As time passed, he was less and less capable of taking care of himself. In Minneapolis, he had made his own bed, seen to his own laundry, fixed his own breakfast. On the rare occasions when they had dinner at home, he helped Caroline with the dishes. Now Helen did all these things, and by the time they moved to Nashville in June, 1976, she had to bathe him. She had help, a woman who came to clean. She still swam and rode and in other ways amused herself, but she had her share of work to do. And she knew, as none of the rest of us could know, what Allen's ventures into the world cost him.

In 1971, Cleanth Brooks organized a panel to discuss Allen's "A Southern Mode of the Imagination" at the Modern Language Association (MLA) meeting in Chicago. Allen wanted to hear what was said about him, and he also wanted to talk to Morton Weisman who had bought the Swallow Press and moved it from Denver to Chicago. Swallow published Allen's *Collected Essays*. Weisman had brought out *Essays of Four Decades* in 1969, and he wanted to become Allen's principal publisher. He was trying to get the rights to Allen's poetry from Scribner's, and he wanted an option on whatever Allen might write next.

Allen rode the bus to Nashville on the day before we went to Chicago. When he arrived, he was firmly established in his role of worried and aging husband, but he rose from his nap at our house the charming *bon vivant* and man of letters. He drank and ate well. He allowed our daughter Pam, who had a new camera, to photograph him from a dozen angles. He complimented our son Larry who passed through the living room in a tuxedo. He said he liked to see young people in formal clothes and wished Larry a happy evening and a future filled with joyous occasions. The next day on the plane we talked a little about his essay that the panel was to consider. Then he turned his attention to his business with Swallow. They were going to offer him a contract, but the terms had not been discussed. As if Helen had never mentioned her need for money, as if none of their concerns about the children's future had ever been voiced, Allen said, "I'm going to ask them for a thousand dollars. They'd give me more, but I want just enough to prove that the contract is serious. I don't want to feel that I'm in their debt."

"But if you could get more," I said.

"No. I only want a thousand."

I was on Cleanth's panel, but my main duty was to be Allen's batman. At O'Hare, I got our baggage. Then we found the entrance where Weisman and Michael Anania, the Swallow poetry editor, were waiting in a black Mercedes. I was unaccustomed to such luxury, but Allen, who had some very rich friends, took it quite in stride. While Anania put our bags in the trunk, Allen entered the car with a lively step and sank into the leather upholstery as if he never traveled any other way. He was such a good conversationalist that even his small talk was entertaining. His comments on the same things that the rest of us would have talked about—the buildings near the airport, the brightness of the day, the traffic on the freeway—were endowed with his mild irony, his tolerant disapproval of the modern world. At the hotel, he thanked Mort Weisman for the ride. Then he said, "As soon as Walter gets me checked in, I'm going to take a nap. I'll meet you at the cocktail hour. In the meantime, if you want to, you can talk to Walter."

Allen's expansive manner had made my role in his affairs seem more important than it was. Mort said he would indeed like to talk to me, and by the time I got to the bar, he and Michael had been joined by a third person who worked for Swallow, Durrett Wagner. We got down to business as soon as our drinks had been served. Mort said that he admired Allen and his work and wanted to be his publisher, but Swallow was a small house and he did not know whether he could meet Allen's terms.

"I don't think you'll have any trouble," I said. "He won't ask for much."

The people from Swallow glanced at each other. They appeared to be encouraged, but were still uneasy since no figure had been named.

"Do you know how much?" Mort said.

"I think he's going to ask you for a thousand dollars."

Weisman was astonished, but pleased. "I could give him more."

"Well," I said, "talk to Allen."

Later in the afternoon, the conversation was repeated, this time with Allen speaking for himself. "No," Allen said, "all I want is a thousand dollars, just to make sure we have a contract." Mort accepted this, and he began to tell Allen how he was going to try to get the rights to Allen's poems from Scribner's. Allen had another drink, smoked a few more cigarettes. He was as far away from Sewanee and anxieties about the future as if he had been on the other side of the world. Rested after his nap, he told stories of the time he had worked for Holt: his expense account had been twice his salary, and books he had edited had been, he said, among the few that paid their own way. This conversation, the men from Swallow could relate to. They told publishing stories of their own. Soon it was time for Allen and me to meet some other people for dinner, during which his happy mood persisted. He engaged all present with his charm.

Though he had drunk a lot and smoked more, the next morning Allen was still energetic. We joined Cleanth and Bill Wimsatt and Louis Rubin for breakfast. Perhaps because we were all southerners, we began to talk of the Civil

War. Wimsatt's family had owned the house at Appomattox where Lee had surrendered to Grant, and Bill took the defeat of the Confederate army personally. The house had been vandalized by Federal soldiers seeking souvenirs, and much of the furniture had been stolen. Allen, remembering work he had done fifty years before, spoke of Stonewall Jackson and Jefferson Davis, praising one and damning the other. He and Bill lamented the loss of Jackson which, they thought, had caused the loss at Gettysburg, which in turn had led to the loss of the war. They had not yet said that they wished the South had won, but they were tending strongly in that direction, when R. W. B. Lewis, who along with Louis and Allen and Cleanth and me, was to be on the Tate panel, sat down at our table. Lewis reprimanded Allen and Bill for their Confederate fervor; he said the southern cause had been corrupt and the war had ended as it should have.

Bill and Allen were sitting across from each other and both of them stood up. Bill was big, easily six and a half feet tall, and heavy. He made Allen appear to be even smaller than he was, but he did not surpass Allen in indignation.

"You don't know anything about it," Allen said to Dick Lewis.

"Absolutely nothing," Wimsatt added. "Don't try to discuss it."

Dick was surprised into silence. Allen and Bill sat down and, as if there had been no interruption, they continued to lament the demise of the Confederate South.

The panel, which was held in a large room at the Palmer House, was well attended. Allen had asked to be allowed to make the final statement in our discussion, and since the panel was entirely composed of his friends, he had nothing to do except sit and look modestly pleased while we complimented him. We praised the essay in particular and his accomplishment in general. He had, we said, delineated the causes of the southern renascence better than any other critic. We went beyond the essay under examination to speak of his views on southern religion and culture and on the qualities of the human imagination. We praised his role in the development of the New Criticism and his practice thereof. As we always did when we appeared together in those days, Louis Rubin and I argued about whether the southern renascence had ended, but there was no argument about Allen's achievement. The panel joined in celebration of his distinguished career.

Allen said what, in my experience, he always said when he was acclaimed in public: that our discussion had come closer to stating the true intention of his work than anything else that had ever been spoken or written about him. He said the same thing at his seventy-fifth birthday celebration at Sewanee and when he received a gold medal from Aquinas College in Nashville and to several critics who had written essays about him. He was extravagant, but I think not disingenuous. He appreciated praise and wanted to respond to it; in the euphoria of the moment, he meant what he said.

Early in the afternoon, Mort Weisman sent a young man to take us to the airport. We got into the Mercedes, Allen in front, I in back, and set out for O'Hare. The day was cold. It was cold in the car, and Allen asked for heat. Our driver, unfamiliar with the controls of the Mercedes, began to press buttons. The radio came on and then the tape player. The windshield wipers flapped back and forth, the dome light glowed. Finally the sunroof began to open. "That's all right," Allen said. "I think we can do without heat until we get to the airport." And so we did, riding mostly in silence with our coats buttoned tightly and our collars pulled up. At O'Hare, I found a place for Allen to sit while I got our boarding passes and checked our bags. I asked him if he wanted a drink.

"No," he replied, "let's go on to our gate." A weariness that was more than simply being tired, began to possess him. We had left the world of letters when we stepped out of the Palmer House. We were on our way home.

While we waited to board, I recalled as well as I could all the good things that had been said about him by the members of the panel. He cheered up briefly, but on the plane, he was mostly silent, and again he declined a drink. At Nashville, Helen and Jane were waiting for us. Knowing that we would not be fed on the plane, we had planned to have dinner at the airport. We did, but it was a dreary affair. There were two restaurants at the Nashville terminal then, one decent as such restaurants go, the other plain and unappetizing. Helen insisted that we go to the latter to save money. No drinks were served here. We sat in a booth and ate the poor food—I remember the frozen green beans as being particularly bad—and Allen's weariness increased and his breath became labored. He took only a few bites and the rest of us were soon through. Twenty-four hours earlier, he had been having a drink at a Chicago restaurant. Twelve hours ago, he had stood up with Bill Wimsatt in defense of the Confederacy. Now he was ready to get in his car and return home. I put his bags in the trunk. Jane kissed him good-by. We shook hands.

He said, "I couldn't have made it without you, Walter."

"Oh, yes, you could," I replied. "You were the star of the show."

Helen was already behind the wheel, but for a moment, Allen hesitated, and in the silence, I could hear his rasping, shallow breath.

"Well," he said, "good-by again."

He walked slowly to the car and got in. Helen drove away.

V

IN *The Strange Children*, Caroline's *roman a clef*, Lucy, who is Nancy, says of her mother and father who are Caroline and Allen, "None of their friends ever quite suited them. You would think they were crazy about a person but the minute he turned his back they were on him, tearing him to pieces." This seemed to me to be more true of Allen than of Caroline. He said bad things about everybody, and when you listened to him denigrate Red or Malcolm Cowley or Caroline or Hart Crane—for him, the dead were as fair subjects as the living—you knew that when you were gone and the next visitor came, he would talk about you in the same way; he did not reserve his criticism for the famous. But this was all right, because it seemed to me that even when he was saying the worst things about his friends, he still maintained his loyalty to them. Once in Minneapolis, he was castigating Mr. Ransom. He was finding flaws in the poetry which he said were manifestations of flaws in the person who had written it. But when someone else tried to join in the criticism, Allen changed sides and came to Mr. Ransom's defense. "It's all right for us to talk about John," he said to me later, "but I won't have him attacked by outsiders."

Andrew was one of Allen's closest friends. They had met in New York in 1927, and for the next decade they visited each other and shared whatever they had. Andrew wrote part of *Bedford Forrest* at Benfolly; Caroline worked on *The Garden of Adonis* at the Lytle house in Monteagle. Andrew and Edna spent a summer with Caroline and Allen at Princeton; the Tates lived for a while with the Lytles in New Orleans. Allen lent Andrew money, and Andrew offered to share with Allen the largesse of George Haight, his generous, Hollywood friend. One of the reasons Allen retired to Sewanee was to be near Andrew, and those of us who knew them well and spent afternoons and evenings listening to them talk learned much from both of them.

Allen was more cosmopolitan, more elegantly educated than Andrew. In a way that would have been impossible for Andrew, Allen had come close to making himself all things to all people, not by dissembling, but by utilizing his exquisite sense of the moods and prejudices of others. He had all but lost his southern accent while Andrew, who insisted on being from the South wherever he went, cultivated his and used it to good effect when he told his off-color, backwoods stories. One was a poet, the other a novelist, though Allen had written a novel too. And their criticism was as different, or appeared to be, as the genres in which they worked. Allen's range was greater: he wrote about criticism, poetry and fiction while Andrew examined novels and stories. Allen was a better classicist, a better student of the history of criticism, and most important of all, a better theologian. When Allen retired to Sewanee, both men were professed Christians and both accepted the creeds. But Andrew had read deeply in Jung: he inclined to see his faith in terms of myth. Allen had been a neo-Scholastic and therefore an Aristotelian before he had become a Catholic. A two-thousand-year-old system of orderly thought informed his work.

As important as these differences were, their basic views of life and the world were the same. Allen's return to the South was spiritual as well as physical. He had come back to the country Andrew had never left, and though he cherished his past, the places he had lived and the friends he had made, his memories, when he was at peace to indulge them, were often about Kentucky and Tennessee, his youth and his childhood. When I visited him in Minneapolis in 1951, he

70

read aloud the opening section of "The Swimmers," which he was working on then, and he talked about a lynching he had seen when he was a child that had been a basis for his poem. This conversation explored technique, the translation of experience into poetry, the struggle for economy and meaning: it was more literary than reminiscent. But once he had moved to Sewanee, his talk often centered on the past itself—his mother and father, his days at Vanderbilt, his first year in Paris—without regard to how he had turned memory into image in his poetry. He and Andrew had written about the Civil War at the same time in their lives, both of them partisans of the Confederacy and enemies of Jefferson Davis. Allen had taught Edna at Southwestern in Memphis before Andrew met her in New Orleans and married her. Their lives touched, their affections crossed in a thousand places, and like people long married who have learned and rejoiced and suffered together, they seemed to carry on a single conversation that could be taken up effortlessly after a night's or a year's interruption.

Allen talked about Andrew of course. As Lucy said of her father in Caroline's novel, he was unable not to talk about any person who ever lived. In 1923, he wrote to Donald Davidson, "If Jesus Christ should come upon earth and present me with a poem I sincerely thought inferior, I would tell him *just that* to his teeth," which is first of all a statement of literary integrity, but the terms in which Allen couched it set the tone he used when he talked about all his friends. He said that Andrew was provincial, that he wasted time when he should have been writing, that he needed to entertain students, as he did almost daily, to sustain his ego. Even when Allen was finding increasing comfort in turning his thoughts backward, he criticized Andrew for not keeping up with the times. This was ordinary stuff, the sort of thing he said about all of us, and Jane and I were so accustomed to hearing it that we did not notice immediately when his criticism grew harsher and his tone changed.

Or rather, we did notice, but it seemed that Allen's conversation was in general more vituperative, that he said meaner things about everybody, which we blamed on his grieving over Michael and on Helen's desire for money with which she tormented him as well as herself. Then we saw that he was talking more about Andrew than about anybody else; and Bill Ralston and the Harrisons, whom he had seldom mentioned in the past, were occupying his attention. Finally, he said that something was wrong with Andrew, that he had changed and grown cold and distant in his relationship with Allen. Allen feared that their friendship was at an end. We asked Allen what the trouble was. He told us, as he told everyone else who asked, that he did not know.

Allen talked about Andrew's disaffection to everyone who came to see him: the Cheneys, Monroe and Betty Spears, Madison Jones, Robert Daniel, Peter Taylor, and dozens of others who lived at or passed through Sewanee. He said that Andrew had stopped inviting him and Helen to his house except for big parties. Andrew had stopped coming to see him. Ralston and the Harrisons were saying that he and Helen had rejected Andrew's friendship and were ungrateful for the many favors Andrew and they had done for him and Helen. Most of us who heard all this were friends of Andrew as well as of Allen, and the rift between them made us sad and uncomfortable. The hope that we might make peace between them was in the back of all our minds, but while Allen claimed not to know what had ruptured their friendship, for a long time Andrew would not talk about the matter at all.

Finally, Andrew said that Helen had spoken to him "through the screen." He had gone to the Tates' house one afternoon as he often did to spend the cocktail hour with Allen, and Helen would not let him come in. She told Jane later that Andrew's visits were an inconvenience to her. This was in 1969. She was pregnant with Benjamin and had John and Allen to take care of. She was orderly by nature, and adhering to domestic routine was one of the ways she coped with the death of Michael. Allen had been surprised that on the morning of Michael's funeral, she had gone about her familiar tasks, fixing breakfast, making beds, straightening up the house and loading the dishwasher. Housework was

72

still important to her, but she was tired too, and by the time Andrew usually arrived, she wanted to feed John and Allen and get John to bed. When Andrew came, she either had to invite him to dinner or feed John and wait until Andrew left before she fed Allen.

Andrew might have understood her position, but she did not know how to explain it to him. In the first place, and above all else, when he came to her door, she should have invited him in. She should have taken him into her living room and asked him to sit down. He would not have liked being told not to visit Allen at the cocktail hour or not to visit without an invitation or whatever Helen might have told him. The nuances of her message and the words she used would have been of the utmost importance. But before any subtleties of language could affect anything, she had to observe formalities that were crucial in Andrew's code of personal relationships and of which Helen was ignorant. Andrew tried to allow for the fact that she came from Minnesota, but he was deeply offended.

Andrew told of being sent away from the door by Helen a few times to a few people, then he stopped. Later, when he was asked what had happened between him and Allen and Helen, he said, as I remarked earlier, that they could not forgive him for their having been at his house when Michael died, and I think this is a part of the truth. For Helen and Allen, after the funeral, there came the time for speculation. What if they had not been at Andrew's that night? they wondered. What if Michael had not fallen, or the sitter had been more alert or Eleanor Harrison had known to turn Michael over on his stomach? They could think of a dozen, a hundred ways in which their child might have been saved, but the facts of the case were immutable: they had been where they had been and what had happened had happened. Their burden was too great for them to bear without striking out at someone, so they struck out at Andrew and Bill Ralston and the Harrisons.

It was typical of the way he still possesses those who loved him that early in 1987, eight years after Allen's death, an hour before Howard Nemerov was to receive the first

Aiken Taylor Award for Modern American Poetry, conversation in Susan and George Core's living room turned not to the honor Howard was about to receive, but to memories of Allen. Along with Howard, Betty and Monroe Spears were there, and Jane and I and Andrew. Mostly we told each other stories that all of us already knew with now and then a fresh detail emerging. At one point, Jane and Andrew spoke privately. "He was always a difficult man," Andrew said.

"Oh, yes, he was," Jane replied, and this seemed to set Andrew's mind at ease. Throughout the years of Allen's and Andrew's enmity, we had tried to maintain our friendship with both of them, but at times it no doubt seemed to Andrew that we sided with Allen.

Andrew told Jane that Allen had once come to see him at the *Sewanee Review* office, apparently in an effort to heal the breach between them. He sat down but had little to say. Allen may have thought that the gesture he was making merely by presenting himself to Andrew would be sufficient to restore their friendship. But for Andrew the friendship was over. "I told him," Andrew said, "that we had had forty years of affection for each other that I cherished. Now we ought to let things drop between us, remember what we had had, and be grateful for it. But that was not Allen's way of doing things."

Indeed it was not Allen's way, particularly when he was not writing and not reading as much as he once had and there was little to occupy his mind beyond Helen's complaining. He seized on his dispute with Andrew as an antidote to boredom, and having the Harrisons next door multiplied his opportunities for malice. Charles Harrison was Andrew's loyal friend to whom he had dedicated *The Hero with the Private Parts*. Like Allen, Charles had more time at his disposal than he had responsibilities to discharge. He taught his classes, read enough to keep up in his field, worked in his garden, and listened to classical music. The Harrisons were childless, as I have said, but they had a dog, as did the Tates. The Tates' dog Yorick barked when the doorbell rang, but otherwise was quiet and well behaved; and though I saw the Harrisons' dog only occasionally, it seemed to be of the same amiable disposition. The two dogs got along with each other, but Yorick dug a hole in Charles' garden, and the Harrisons' dog tore up a pair of John Tate's shoes.

John's shoes became celebrated throughout Sewanee. Allen and Helen said they were new. Charles and Eleanor said the shoes were almost worn out. Allen and Helen said the dog had taken the shoes from the Tates' screened porch. Charles and Eleanor said that John had removed his shoes and abandoned them in front of the Harrisons' house. Finally, the Harrisons said the shoes were not torn up at all, but simply misplaced and later found. Bill Ralston took up the cause and spread the Harrisons' version of the story. Helen was as vigorous as Allen in denouncing the Harrisons' dog, and she emphasized the high cost of children's shoes and of living in general. She showed Jane what was left of the shoes. Andrew, having by this time said all he intended to say about himself and Allen, kept his silence.

To the best of my knowledge, the last time Andrew was in Allen's house was after the christening of Benjamin. Unlike the twins, Benjamin remained full term in his mother's womb. On the night Ben was born in December, 1969, Henry Arnold, a member of the Sewanee English department who lived across the street from the Tates, drove Helen and Allen to the old St. Thomas Hospital in Nashville where Helen was delivered without complication. The fast drive from Sewanee with Helen in labor and his stint in the father's waiting room had lifted Allen's spirits briefly, but the next day, with the excitement over, he was depressed. On her way to visit Helen, Jane found him in the corridor of the maternity ward. She saw a plume of smoke rising from behind a potted plant. Allen was sitting half crouched beside the greenery, his forehead resting on the heel of the hand that held his cigarette.

"Allen," Jane said.

He did not speak or look up.

She put her hand on his shoulder. "Allen?"

"Yes, Jane," he said mournfully.

75

Within a day or two, he would be himself again, proud of his virility in spite of his uncertain future, basking in the congratulations of his friends and railing against Andrew. But for the moment, he seemed to be looking at himself with an objectivity that he seldom achieved; he appeared to see what his adventurous life had brought him to. Less than two years before, at Vanderbilt Hospital, he had made a boast of his paternity. Now being a new father had brought him close to despair.

Jane waited, her hand still on his shoulder. He said, "Jane, I have two little boys and they are mine, all mine."

Fannie and Lon Cheney spent the night before Benjamin's christening with Andrew, and Allen who frequently lost his civility but never abandoned his manners, felt obliged to invite Andrew to the luncheon that followed the ceremony. There were enough of us present that we did not have to take places at the table or engage in a common conversation. Allen sat on one side of the room; Andrew sat on the other. A few times as they went for food or drink, they exchanged remarks, but the strained relationship between them infected us all. I had known both of these men for more than half my life and I loved and respected them. I could not remember a time before that day that I was not happy to be in their company. But now I, and I think most others who were present, wished we were somewhere else. The cold formality with which they treated each other validated the division between them.

This occurred early in 1970. In less than two years, Andrew would have to retire as editor of the *Sewanee Review* and a faculty committee soon began to search for a new editor. Allen had no official status on the committee, but he was determined to have a voice in naming Andrew's successor. He was motivated partly by his concern that the *Review* be well edited, partly by his animus for Andrew. But mainly, he was doing what he had always done: tending to business that was not necessarily his; participating in whatever literary work or controversy he could discover.

Andrew's position was complicated by his loyalty to Bill Ralston. The editorship of the *Review* was a full-time academic appointment. At his option, the new editor could teach part-time and have an assistant editor who would also teach part-time, or he could teach less and assume full editorial responsibility for the magazine. It was generally believed that Andrew wanted Bill as his successor. If Bill were not appointed, Andrew wanted an editor who would keep Bill as his assistant. Otherwise, Bill, who had no degree in English, but who was educated as a theologian, would find his position on the Sewanee faculty in jeopardy. Andrew and Bill had friends on the search committee, including Charles Harrison, but they had no majority; and Allen, even when he was stricken with emphysema and nagged daily about money, was a seasoned and formidable academic politician. Furthermore, he was not hampered by having to carry a candidate for assistant editor on his coattails.

Allen always pursued his ends with great daring. In this case, his method was simply to offer the job to people of whom he approved, though, of course, the job was not his to offer. Not wanting to let grass grow under his feet, he sometimes offered the editorship to two or three people at once, each of whom was led to believe that he was the only candidate—which broke some hearts but dismayed the opposition. Innocent aspirants to the job—many of whom were utterly unqualified—checked their mailboxes several times a day and waited by their telephones. Persons whom Andrew was courting would hear that the job had been filled. By the time one rumor had been laid to rest, Allen would have offered the position to someone else, and the confusion would begin all over again. Allen's spirits rose. His eyes glittered as he denigrated Andrew's candidates. He smiled at the prospect of Bill Ralston's having to leave Sewanee. But in the spring of 1973, as soon as the committee announced the appointment of George Core, who was Allen's final candidate, Allen began to find fault with George.

First, he was annoyed with George and Susan for being

77

late to a reception in George's honor. The Cores had driven up from Athens where George was winding up his work with the University of Georgia Press. George got to the party at the appointed hour, but Susan had to drive to Franklin, Tennessee, seventy-five miles from Sewanee, where the Cores had friends who would care for their children. She had offered not to come at all, but Leah Reis, whose husband Brindley had been on the search committee, assured Susan the party would still be going when she got back to Sewanee and urged her to attend. When Susan finally got to the reception, she was met on the sidewalk not only by Leah who was waiting for her, but by Charles Harrison who was grumpily departing.

"You needn't go in," Charles said to Susan. "You're too late for your own party. The party's over."

Inside, Susan found Andrew and Allen standing as far away from each other as they could get, each surrounded by his own friends. A somewhat nonplussed neutral segment of the faculty drifted between them. Allen was angry because he conceived, correctly, that Susan's tardiness and her and George's separate arrivals would give Ralston and Harrison ammunition to use against him.

George compounded what to Allen was a bad start by not moving to Sewanee at the beginning of th: summer. George had reasons, all of them personal, for staying a while longer in Athens. There was also some delay on the part of Sewanee officials in finding adequate housing for George's family. Perhaps of most importance, Andrew had one more issue of the magazine to edit. He still occupied, or at least frequented, the *Sewanee Review* office. He had not wanted to retire and he had not wanted George to succeed him. George perhaps doubted that he and Andrew could profitably share an office. He drove to Sewanee every week or so to pick up manuscripts and correspondence that he worked on at home. His not being on campus was widely criticized by Ralston and Harrison. Since George had been Allen's candidate, Allen had to defend him. But he damned George too for not coming on to Sewanee and putting the criticism to rest.

78

George did not come, and typically, Allen, sensing a weakness in his own position, attacked. He was under the impression that the Summer, 1973, issue of the *Review* would be Andrew's last. When the magazine appeared with no mention of the change in editorship and no welcome offered to the new editor, Allen wrote to Andrew denigrating the contents of recent issues of the *Review* and reprimanding him for bad manners in not having wished George well. Andrew did not reply. Then, discovering that Andrew's tenure had one more issue to run, Allen wrote Andrew an apology of sorts. He still believed that George should be welcomed to the magazine, but he was sorry for having been mistaken about when Andrew would retire. Andrew never saw the letter. It was returned to Allen still sealed with REFUSED. RETURN TO SENDER stamped on the envelope.

Nothing Andrew could have done would have irritated Allen more. A few days after Allen got his letter back, Jane and I went to his house to get him and Helen for lunch at the Sewanee Inn. As soon as we moved into the living room, Allen said, "I've got something to show you."

"What?"

"Oh, no," he said, "not here." He glanced at John and Benjamin as if whatever it was should not be unveiled in their presence. "I'll show you at lunch."

Even after we got to our table at the Sewanee Inn, he delayed. Then he said, "I wrote a letter to Andrew apologizing for not knowing he had another issue to edit. Now look at this."

He brought the letter out of his inside coat pocket, looked at it for a moment as if he were rereading the address and the message stamped on the envelope, then passed it over to Jane and me. It was still sealed.

"That's Ralston's doing," Allen said. "Andrew wouldn't have thought of it."

I was inclined to agree, but there was no way to be sure.

"I don't know what to do," Allen said. "You see, he won't communicate with me. What do you think I should do?"

I did not know, and Allen's anger was compounded by his

frustration over not knowing either. His feud with Andrew furnished much of the excitement in his life. How was it to be continued, if Andrew refused to read his letters?

We soon found out. During the summer of 1973, Bill Ralston, having been told that he could not continue as a member of the Sewanee English department unless he got more graduate education, moved to Eureka Springs, Arkansas. Several years before, the Reverend Howard Foland had bought land there, named his domain Hillspeak, and had begun, first, the Episcopal Book Club and then a quarterly, the *Anglican Digest*. Father Foland's book and magazine operation had grown, he had aged, and he brought Bill to Arkansas as his possible successor. In some respects, Father Foland could not have made a better choice. Bill is bright and decently educated. He writes well, he had editorial experience, and his theological orthodoxy was consonant with Father Foland's own religious views.

Bill did not stay in Arkansas, but while he was there, he sent Allen a condemnatory letter. He quoted Stravinsky's judgment of a critic: that his work was a "foul supperation of gratuitous malice." He said Allen fit this description. He reminded Allen of the *Inferno*, of the place Dante had reserved in Hell for traitors to friends, and he told Allen that to be such a traitor was a pitiful way to come to the end of his life. He congratulated Allen on having managed to secure the appointment of a new editor of the *Sewanee Review* who did not sufficiently value his appointment to come to Sewanee. He said that he did not know why Allen had done the things he had done, and that he was afraid for Allen. The letter was couched in terms of vilification that neither Andrew nor Allen had ever used. Bill had sent it from Arkansas where, Allen assumed, it had been written without Andrew's knowledge or advice or collaboration. Allen was hurt, but he decided not to respond.

Bill's letter was dated September 1, 1973. A month or six weeks later, Andrew's final issue of the *Sewanee Review* carried a thirty-nine-page essay by Ralston. Dedicated to Charles Harrison and accepted for publication by Andrew, the essay used more veiled and civilized language but also consigned Allen to hell. It was extraordinary in its subject as well as in its length. Entitled "That Old Serpent," it was a fairly conventional exploration of the creation of the world, the fall of man, his redemption by Christ, his relationship to God, and his freedom under the terms of his creation and redemption. Bill's piece was literary only in the sense that he quoted poetry and referred to familiar characters such as Iago and Cordelia to make some of his points. He defined human happiness in terms of our communion with God and with each other. He saw hell as the rejection of God and an absorption with self. Nothing could have been more traditional, and nowhere in his text did he mention Allen Tate's name. But he drew a clear distinction between the saved and the damned and he concluded his essay with two quotations, one representing the right way, one the wrong: one by Eliot, the other by Tate.

Bill, who had known Allen well and who had appeared to love Helen and Allen as Andrew and Charles had loved them at one time, was conscious of the irony of this juxtaposition. He had seen the photograph of Eliot, inscribed to Allen, that hung in Allen's study and later in his bedroom. He had been assistant editor of the *Review* when Allen had collected and edited the essays for the special issue on Eliot. He had heard Allen speak of Eliot as one of his two masters in the art of poetry. Bill was using the work of Allen's old friend and teacher to damn Allen. Ralston cited lines from the last section of "Little Gidding" as a proper description of Christian submission and reconciliation. Then he printed the passage from "Ode to the Confederate Dead" that speaks of setting up "the grave in the house" and, more significantly, of the serpent in the mulberry bush.

Now the lines Allen had quoted to Andrew and Andrew had quoted to him, innocent as they seem out of the context of Bill's paper, were used to consign Allen to the lowest level of humanity that Bill had already described in some detail. The argument between Allen and Andrew and his friends that had been conducted in a kind of privacy was now made

81

public in harsher and more judgmental terms than had been used before. This was its climax. Ralston was gone. Andrew continued to keep his silence. Allen, perhaps bored, at last, by the whole proceeding and feeling a little battered, turned his mind to other things.

VI

✍

ALMOST EVERYBODY who came to Sewanee in the fall of 1974 knew more about Allen's past than Helen did. From November 14 to November 16 of that year, the University of the South held a conference, organized largely by George Core, to celebrate Allen's seventy-fifth birthday and to praise his work. There were some good papers and an interesting panel discussion and some very interesting informal conversations—not only among the participants, but among the distinguished guests who had come not so much to hear the program as to honor Allen. Among those present were Cleanth Brooks, Denis Donoghue, Louis Rubin, Lewis Simpson, William Jay Smith, Eudora Welty, William Meredith, Joseph Frank, Howard Nemerov, Francis Ferguson, Doris Grumbach, and Radcliffe Squires whose presence must have been a comfort to Allen. Three years earlier, Radcliffe had published *Allen Tate: A Literary Biography* in which he had dutifully listed Allen's marriages and divorces, but had told nothing else. There was no mention of the way Allen had abandoned Caroline for Isabella and abandoned Isabella for Helen, and no hint of his many affairs. By the time of the birthday celebration, Helen had begun to hear references to Allen's past infidelities, and she was upset by them, but she did not yet suspect how many women there had been in his life.

The festivities started on the afternoon of the fourteenth

and that evening, at a well attended banquet, Allen's friends were invited publicly to reminisce. Allen sat in uneasy glory while his fellow poets and critics told stories about him. Following Radcliffe's discreet example, none of them mentioned Caroline or Isabella, but their anecdotes created an ambience that included those earlier wives and a past of which Helen had not been a part. The man who was her husband was not the person whose memory was being evoked. She had never really known the old Allen—the poet while he was still a practicing poet, the critic while he still wrote criticism, the man of letters when he exerted the power of his position in the literary world. She may have felt isolated from the Allen being described that night and from the friends who were describing him. And as Allen had come to know by now, no account of his past wit or achievement would endear her to the life he had led.

Around 1970, John Tyree Fain, who was later joined in the project by Dan Young, asked Allen's permission to edit and publish the literary correspondence between him and Donald Davidson. Assuming a position that he was to maintain until he died whenever questions were raised about publishing his letters or writing his biography, Allen demurred, but he did not say no. He wanted the publicity and any money the book might earn, but he feared what ghosts the letters might awaken. He had met Mr. Davidson in 1920. They had been good friends and written to each other often during the twenties and thirties and less frequently during the forties and fifties and sixties. There was plenty of material to make a book and most of it was about literature, but even Allen with his prodigious memory could not recall every letter he had written or what he might have disclosed about his personal life. Characteristically, he fretted aloud for a long time before he was willing to say what was truly worrying him.

First he said he did not want to have any of his letters published. Then he said that if they were to be published, they should all be published at the same time—the complete letters or a selection therefrom rather than a particular correspondence. He said he was not sure Tyree and Dan were the people to edit his letters, by which he meant he was not sure he could trust them not to bring to light something that would embarrass him or make his life with Helen more difficult. Coming closer to his real concern, but still dissimulating, he said that he was afraid the letters would offend Mr. Ransom. "John was the oldest member of our group," he explained. "He thought of himself as head of the Fugitives. Don and I were a little in rebellion against his authority."

"Maybe you ought to put off publishing any of your letters for a while," I suggested.

"I think I will, Walter," he said. "That's good advice."

But the next time I saw him, a few weeks later, we had the same conversation. Even as he claimed not to have decided what he would do, Dan and Tyree got copies of the correspondence and began to edit it.

He took the same approach to his biography. "Someone's going to write it," he said, which was obviously true. He said he did not want one; clearly he did, but not one that would tell the whole truth. The situation had its comic aspect. No one, I suppose, knew about all of Allen's adventures and misadventures; but almost everybody who had known Allen before he married Helen knew about enough of them to understand how strongly his libido had influenced his life. Allen was aware of this, and as he demonstrated when his and Helen's children were born, he was not averse to having his friends talk about his sexual prowess. But Helen was appalled at the notion that a biographer would include this subject in a book her sons would eventually read. And almost as much as he desired the public notice that a biography would bring him, Allen desired to keep what remained of his domestic peace.

Following Twayne's publication of Ferman Bishop's biography of Allen in 1967 Louis Rubin, thinking that Allen deserved better than he had received in this volume, offered to write the Tate biography after Allen's death. Allen agreed and told Louis that he would appoint Louis his official biographer in his will. But as time passed, Allen began to fret over what Louis—or anyone else—might disclose about his escapades with women, and he urged Louis to write the biography while he was still alive to help. Louis did not want Allen's assistance, and when it became clear that not only Allen but Helen too would be looking over his shoulder, Louis withdrew. Allen then set out to find an author who would allow him and Helen to censor what he wrote. Allen's method was similar to the one he had used when a new editor of the *Sewanee Review* was to be chosen: he would pick a candidate and say the candidate had applied for the job. He named several people, but for a while, no one who suited Allen was willing to undertake the biography on Allen's terms.

While the search for an author continued, Allen worked out his defense. Since even in his most brazen posture, he could not claim that his life had been pure, he searched for ways to confuse the issue and to put the best light on what could not be denied. For example, he said that he resigned as editor of the *Sewanee Review* late in 1945 because of his impending divorce from Caroline. This was part of the truth, though it seems more likely that Alexander Guerry, vice-chancellor of the university at the time, dismissed him because of other scandals. Caroline had left Allen not of her own volition, but because after months of quarreling, he had ordered her to leave. He was having an affair with the wife of a Sewanee professor, a fact that was well known on campus. He told his friends that he was really in love with the wife of a faculty member at the University of Virginia, with whom, he said, he was also having an affair. His name, in 1944, was linked to the names of other women as well, as it had often been before and would be in the future. But the question of the biography was under discussion in the early 1970s. Allen had been behaving himself since his marriage to Helen; he hoped that time would blur, if not eradicate memories; and he set out to obscure his past. One afternoon when he had come to Nashville without Helen, he said, "When I edited the *Sewanee Review*, somebody spread the story that I was having an affair with Mildred Haun. It wasn't true. But, you see, rumors like that are very persistent."

Mildred had been Allen's editorial assistant, and as he must have remembered, it was she who had started the rumor. She had told Alex Guerry that Allen had seduced her, but even Guerry, annoyed as he was by Allen's indiscreet philandering, could not have believed her. Mildred had come to Vanderbilt from her home in the Tennessee mountains in the thirties, studied under Mr. Ransom and Mr. Davidson and later with Wilbur Schramm at Iowa. A collection of her stories was published in 1940, and she was still pursuing a literary career when she signed on to help Allen in 1944. Mildred was truly a nice person, but she had none of the qualities that Allen's other lovers had. She was homely of face and figure, which would not necessarily have been crucial, except that she was shy and seemingly devoid of the spark and wit and sophistication that most of Allen's mistresses possessed. Even at the end of her life—she died in 1966—when she was living and working in Washington, a part of her was still in the mountains among the people with whom she had been raised. No one who had known her and Allen could possibly believe that romance had ever blossomed between them, and Allen depended on the very absurdity of the idea to cast doubt on rumors of his other indulgences.

This ploy did not work, as Allen must have known that it would not, so he retreated to another line of defense. Since he could hardly claim otherwise, given what was generally known about his courtship of Helen, he admitted that he had not always been true to Caroline and Isabella. He tried to make his infidelities appear to have been mere flirtations and to cast himself in the role of an innocent who was at the mercy of a complicated world. Again on a trip to Nashville without Helen, he said, "Elizabeth Hardwick and I were once close. When we broke up, I suggested that we return the letters we had written each other. She said we could simply burn them. I burned hers to me, but I don't know whether she burned mine to her. It would be bad if she didn't and somebody got hold of them."

"Surely she burned them," I said.

"Well," he said, "if she did, I don't have anything to worry about." He sat back on the couch and smiled as if whatever had happened between him and Elizabeth was the only aspect of his past he needed to concern himself with.

Helen was learning better, and she seemed to change with every new detail she learned of Allen's past. When Jane and I would go to see her and Allen, each time her frown would seem deeper, her voice more shrill. She would indicate to Jane that something new had come to light about Allen, something that should not be made public—though the fact that she finally knew of it was evidence that it was public already—something that her children should never be allowed to learn. Her personality that had changed after the death of Michael now changed again. When she had first married Allen, she had been happy and gentle and, as Allen had said, not brilliant, but pleasant to be around and to talk to. Now she was bitter and filled with complaint; she seemed to distrust Allen's literary friends. Once when the Cowleys were her and Allen's houseguests, Helen grew angry about a story Muriel Cowley told at the dinner table because of a four-letter word the story contained.

I first remember meeting the Cowleys in 1970 at Hollins College where Malcolm was the featured speaker at the spring literary festival and where Muriel's gentle and gentile nature was put to the test. A part of the program that year was a performance of *The Congresswoman* in a translation that exploited Aristophanes' sexual and scatological humor in the blunt language that the sixties had brought into public use. The reaction of the audience interfered with Malcolm's hearing and after some of the most graphic jokes, just as the laughter was subsiding, Malcolm would lean toward Muriel and ask, "What did he say? What did he say?" Muriel would not repeat what he had said. Sometimes she gave Malcolm a bowdlerized version and sometimes she did not answer. This was a funny sequence in which Muriel and later Malcolm saw the humor, and the way Muriel maintained her dignity and good will were indicative of the great lady she is.

The story Muriel told at the Tates'—a story Jane and I heard her tell on another occasion—was mild and funny and required the objectionable word to achieve its effect. Helen took exception to it. She said that such language could not be used in the house where she was rearing her sons. Malcolm also got in trouble with Helen that evening by innocently referring to an early poem by Allen, "The Death of Little Boys." Helen left the table. Allen was deeply embarrassed, as were the Cowleys. They muddled through the rest of the dinner, said goodnight, and went to their rooms, but the incident was not over. The next morning, when it was mercifully time for the Tates to drive the Cowleys to the airport, Helen could not find the keys to her car. She accused Muriel of having hidden them, though the thing Muriel wanted most of all at that moment was to be on her way back to Sherman, Connecticut. The keys were finally located and Allen and the Cowleys made strained conversation on the drive to the airport.

This scene, and others like it involving some of his less-famous friends, must have been very difficult for Allen. Malcolm and Muriel were loyal to him to the end. Malcolm dedicated A Second Flowering "To Allen Tate/Poet and Companion." He and Muriel welcomed any news they could get of Allen and were genuinely pleased to hear of any improvement in his health or of any award he received. Allen could not fully reciprocate. He continued to correspond with Malcolm and doubtless expressed affection in his letters, but in public he felt obliged to be loyal to Helen. When she rehearsed her outrage at the word Muriel had used and persisted in her conviction that Muriel had hidden her car keys, Allen agreed with her and supported her in her accusations. He was too dependent on her to risk annoying her, and when she pared the guest list for the luncheon she was giving during his seventy-fifth birthday celebration, Allen pretended the idea to shrink the party was his.

Their original plan was to entertain everyone connected with the program along with distinguished guests who had come from out of town. Allen issued invitations to the Cores and the Cheneys and various others, but as time for the birthday celebration approached, he began to fret that such a party as he had planned would be too much of an imposition on Helen. He first decided that invitations to those who lived in Sewanee or within fifty miles thereof should be rescinded. This eliminated the Cores, though George had planned the birthday symposium and had done most of the work to organize it. Still the guest list was too large, so the prohibition was extended to include anyone who lived within a hundred miles of Sewanee, which took care of the Cheneys at Smyrna and of those of us who lived in Nashville as well. Allen announced this policy to me and Jane about a week before his birthday. "We're not inviting you," he said, though with his all-but-infallible memory, he must have realized that he had already done so. "The party was getting too big for Helen to handle. We're cutting down on it by not asking the people we see frequently anyway."

He said this with such good humor and sincerity that I found it difficult to be offended. Something in his voice and deep in his eyes seemed to plead a case that he would not dare state. Yet to put it this way is not quite to say how he actually appeared. He was not asking for sympathy. He was not hinting that he had lost control of his life. Rather he seemed to want us to understand that he had had to choose between imposing on us and imposing on Helen, and he had decided, for reasons that we might not comprehend as well as we thought we did, to impose on us.

"You see," he said, "the house is too small to accommodate so many people."

Yes, we said. We saw. We understood.

Allen was not strong enough to sit through the program, but George Core had got copies of the papers for him to read beforehand, and on Saturday night when the formal proceedings were finished, he attended the reception being given in his honor and held court. He settled himself on an antique couch in one of the sitting rooms at the vice-chancellor's house and conscripted a willing Madison Bell, seventeen years old, but already on his way to becoming a novelist, as his majordomo. Madison got him drinks and helped him light his cigarettes and summoned guests singly into Allen's presence. No one questioned this pattern that Allen established. We loitered in conversation with each other until Madison appeared at someone's elbow and said, "Mr. Tate would like to see you now," and that person went to the room where Allen was waiting. As always, after a little whiskey and the stimulation of literary discussion, Allen seemed to have overcome some of his illness and to have shed some of his years—an impression enhanced by the perfect drape of his suit, the starch in his collar, the knot in his tie. That morning I had read a paper on *The Fathers* for which he thanked me. As usual, he said it was the best thing ever written about that book. I knew Allen almost invariably said this about any criticism that praised him, but the paper was fresh in my mind and I wanted to believe that it was good and that Allen meant what he was saying. And perhaps he did. Perhaps for that moment, he was convinced that my paper and those by Louis Rubin and Denis Donoghue and Cleanth Brooks were the most astute interpretations of his work that had ever been developed. Such was the nature of his generosity.

As I talked to Allen that night, I remembered the good things he had said about the bad stories I had taken for him to read when I first visited him and Caroline at Monteagle. He had suggested places I might send the stories for possible publication, and he had written editors on my behalf. He had befriended Cal Lowell and Peter Taylor the same way, and John Berryman and, of course, Ezra Pound, who was himself a great busybody like Allen and helper of those whom he judged to have talent and to need help. All this was and is well known. But I knew that Allen had corresponded with and read manuscripts for and tried to assist writers whose names would never be known and most of whose work would never be printed. Whatever his faults, his devotion to literature was absolute and absolutely selfless.

Some of this had been noted during the panel discussion that had taken place that afternoon and that had gotten off to a slow start when Bill Smith, who spoke first, announced that he did not believe in panel discussions. From the outset, Howard Nemerov had given a typically excellent performance, but for a while, he got scant help. All the participants had been to parties the night before and to Allen's for lunch, and they seemed to take a while to recover themselves. At last, their affection for Allen appeared to energize them. They were all bright and distinguished people and like many of the rest of us present, they were in some way or another, in Allen's debt. This they freely admitted, and they thanked him by praising his services to the cause of literature and his work. "I hear the panel was good," Allen said.

"Yes," I replied, "but none of us did you justice."

The next day, Jane and I went by to see Allen before we started home. He was still excited, but already his usual cares were beginning to weigh on his mind. He still had a worried wife and young children. He needed—or at least was told that he needed—more money than he had or could possibly make in order to provide for their future. Now, for him, it was back to correspondence and whatever writing he could manage, and a few more lectures and readings that he would struggle to get through. I tried to talk to him again about the birthday celebration, but the mood of the night before was gone. He was deeply weary, and the boys who ran from his chair to Helen's and back again made him nervous. He asked them to be quiet and Helen took them out of the room.

Passing through Monteagle on our way to the interstate, I remembered how things had been between Allen and Caroline when I had first met them, and later when I had visited them in Minneapolis. In 1951, when they had occupied separate rooms in Joseph Warren Beach's house, they had seemed reasonably happy. They had spoken the same language and had been interested in the same things: his poetry and her novels and the poetry and novels of their friends. Allen had been anxious to get a card in the mail to T. S. Eliot in time for it to arrive before Christmas, and he and Caroline discussed what presents they ought to get for their grandchildren. Caroline had been fifty-six then and Allen fifty-two. One Friday, when we had all had breakfast together, she remarked that in four more years, she would be sixty and she would no longer be required to keep the days of fast and abstinence prescribed by the church. She did not appear to regret her age, and her acceptance seemed to extend to every facet of her existence. She seemed content with what fate had brought her.

Later, after Allen had left her, she was so bitter that she wrote Tom Mabry, her cousin who lived on a farm in Kentucky and wrote short stories, that she never wanted to see the South again. She refused Tom's offer to send her a country ham. But she managed to put her life back together. After a few years of living in Princeton and commuting to New York to teach, she went to the University of Dallas where Donald and Louise Cowan, who were president and head of the English department respectively, treated her as the distinguished person that she was. She returned to Princeton after Don Cowan retired. She was in poor health toward the end of her life, but she was well cared for by Nancy and loved by her grandchildren, and she outlived Allen.

Indeed, she was very much alive in 1974 when we celebrated Allen's seventy-fifth birthday. And driving down the mountain that Sunday afternoon, I wondered what his life would have been like if he had never left her. This was a silly notion, an impossible dream. The last time I had seen Caroline, her hair was almost white; she had gained weight and her face was sagging. When he was in good health and free to go or stay, Allen could never have endured that. He was not capable of that kind of surrender. On that morning in Minneapolis in 1951, I had been so fascinated by Caroline's gentle ruminations over growing old that I never glanced at Allen, never wondered what might be going through his mind. I know that he said nothing, but five years later he was gone from her for good, and fifteen years later he was married to a girl less than half his age. It was preposterous to think of Allen living out his days with Caroline in Princeton, surrounded by grandchildren, accepting the constrictions that time brings.

VII

AT THE TIME of his birthday celebration, Allen had lived almost a year longer than his doctors had predicted. In October, 1973, sick and short of breath and still refusing to take care of himself, he had delivered the Gauss lectures at Princeton. Our daughter and son-in-law, Pamela and Gordon Chenery, were living in Sewanee, and Allen asked them to drive him to the Nashville airport. Since they had moved to Sewanee, they had seen Allen regularly, but always at his house where he did not have to exert himself, where Helen cared for him and kept his life on schedule. They were surprised at how frail he seemed on the trip down the mountain. At his request, when they reached the airport, Gordon got a wheelchair and pushed him to his gate, and he and Pam waited with him until he boarded his plane. At Princeton, he drank and smoked—he had never stopped, though he claimed to have limited himself to eight cigarettes a day—and when he finished his last lecture, he was taken directly from the auditorium to the hospital.

Nancy, whose husband is a psychiatrist, dealt with the doctors, bought Allen an overcoat and a hat to replace those he had lost or perhaps had not brought with him since October weather is mild in Sewanee, shepherded him onto the plane when he was able to travel, and brought him back to Tennessee. The ulcer that had been troubling him for years had worsened, but it could be treated. His emphysema was irreversible, and most of his capacity to breathe was gone. The doctors at Princeton said that a case of flu or bronchitis or pneumonia would kill him, and that given his weak constitution, he would not likely get through the winter without contracting some kind of respiratory disease. When he got home, he was examined by his Nashville doctors who concurred in the gloomy prognosis, but he was tougher than the physicians or any of the rest of us knew. He endured the damp Sewanee winter without catching even a head cold, and in March, 1974, he was able, though barely, to lecture on Robert Frost at the Library of Congress.

While he considered whether he ought to go to Washington, he talked not only of his own health, but of his dislike for Frost whom he described as "dishonest and overbearing." He referred me to Lawrence Thompson's biography and pointed out that Frost had been cruel to women. There was irony here, of course, but perhaps not as much as those who never knew Allen would imagine. Allen mistreated his wives with his infidelities, and he sometimes raged at Caroline who raged back. But in public, his good manners and his gallantry seldom left him. He was gentle and courteous in a way that, apparently, Frost was not. And putting the poetry aside, which he did not do for one minute, Allen said that he did not want to praise a man who had been rude and inconsiderate. Possibly, Allen was simply jealous of Frost's fame, but that winter, after his collapse at Princeton, he took a harsher than usual view of almost everybody, many who were less renowned than he.

He talked about Red Warren, saying that Red's work had suffered because of its popular success, but he was clearly envious of the money Red had made. Through his diligent correspondence, he kept up with the sales of Red's books and the fees he got for ancillary rights. It seemed unfair to Allen and to Helen that his own writing did not make as much, particularly since, as he put it, Red was already rich and did not need more money. And he complained that Red's letters to him were full of family news and not about literature. Allen repeated his grievances against Dr. Mims and his disappointment in Mr. Davidson's response to them, and he talked about Mr. Davidson and Andrew and their views of the South. He said they were both idolaters who worshiped the Old South, but the Souths that they worshiped were different. Mr. Davidson's South, Allen said, was composed of the plain folk singing ballads in the dog trots of their houses. "There were no blacks in Don's South." He said that Andrew worshiped the plantation South, which seemed to me less accurate than what he had said about Mr. Davidson. Andrew's essay in *I'll Take My Stand*, as well as *The Long Night*, the biography of Forrest, and the stories Andrew liked to tell demonstrated his interest in the plain people too, but he did not idealize them as much as Mr. Davidson had.

Allen missed Andrew's company and said so. "I'd like to see Andrew again."

I hesitated at first, wary of offering to serve as peacemaker. Finally, I said, "Do you want me to tell him that?"

"Well," Allen replied, "well . . . I suppose so." He paused. Then he said, "Maybe I'm too quick to forgive. Others are not as quick to forgive as I am."

A couple of weeks later, when we were on the mountain again, Jane and I called on Andrew. He had invited us to his house immediately when I telephoned to tell him we were in Monteagle, and he received us graciously—too graciously in fact, his manners too perfect, his conversation bereft of the country colloquialisms he ordinarily used with his friends. We had not visited him recently, and he thought, with some justification, that I had taken Allen's side in their argument. I had supported George Core for the editorship of the *Review*, and I had been offended by the reference to Allen in Bill Ralston's essay; but I had never lost my admiration and affection for Andrew. Andrew had just finished *A Wake for the Living*, parts of which had already been published in magazines. Jane lured him into telling some of the stories that were in his book, and this took us into the past and back into our friendship. We sat by the fire and drank out of his silver cups and talked for an hour. Then it was time for us to leave, and the moment seemed propitious.

"Andrew," I said, "I think Allen would like to see you again. I think he wants to make up with you."

We were standing, Jane and I with our backs to the door, but preparing to go out of it. Andrew faced us, still holding an ornate cup that from its appearance might once have served as an altar vessel. He seemed to wince, though the change in his expression was almost imperceptible. There was a brief tightening of his lips, a narrowing of his eyes. Then he said, "No. I can't do that. That's over."

Jane and I tried once or twice more to make peace between him and Allen, and I think the Cheneys tried too. But Andrew had meant what he said to Allen when their friendship ended, and it was never resumed.

As Allen's health declined, he was less and less able to look after himself. By 1975, Helen had to bathe him and one day in September of that year, he turned blue and lost consciousness in the bathtub. Helen revived him, and he was taken to Nashville in an ambulance. When Jane and I saw him at Vanderbilt Hospital that afternoon, he appeared to be very sick. He was breathing oxygen through a mask, and his skin retained a bluish tint that made the blue of his eyes seem faded. He was lying on his back: he lifted his hand in greeting, then let it fall on the sheet. Seeing him then, it was impossible not to remember the dire predictions his doctors had made almost two years before. We feared the worst. But once more he recovered. The next day, Allen's doctors replaced the oxygen mask with the plastic breathing tubes that he would wear constantly during the last few years of his life. In a day or two, these were gone, and a day or two after that he was ready to go home.

This stint in the hospital was different from the time Allen had spent there when he had had his circumcision. Then it had been as if he were holding court for anyone who cared to come. He had gossiped and discussed literature and demonstrated his extraordinary capacity for finding things to talk about and turning any subject into interesting conversation. One afternoon Frank Fletcher, in whose house Allen had stayed when the twins were born, came to see him. Allen induced Frank to talk about his family—his son was about to get married—and when this topic was exhausted, Allen asked Frank where he bought his shirts. "I've always admired your shirts, Frank," Allen said. "They've always seemed to me to be handsome and in good taste."

They were indeed. The one Frank was wearing at that moment was white with blue stripes. It was set off by an expensive silk tie and a blue suit that was perfectly tailored. Frank took the question seriously as I think Allen meant for him to. He named a store and spoke of collar styles and monogramming. The quality of this scene is difficult to recapture. What occurred was small talk exquisitely conducted. Allen was seventy-six and Frank had been a year ahead of him in college. They were old men who had led interesting lives: Frank had been a diplomat as well as a businessman. As they talked, I got the sense that throughout all both of them had done, shirts had been important. After Frank left, Allen apologized for having pursued such a long discussion of haberdashery, but he had enjoyed it, and there was no need for him to make excuses. His conversational genius had inspired Frank and I had been fascinated with Allen's performance.

Now as Allen recuperated, there was no talk about shirts and not much about literature. He was still courteous; he welcomed his visitors and attempted to converse with them, but he seemed tired in a way that he had never been before. He lay on his back and asked us to stand at the foot of his bed so he could see us. He asked me—and several other people—to find him a copy of *Two Little Confederates*, a book he remembered from his childhood: he had been thinking about it and thought he might like to write an essay on it. The doctors and nurses treated him as the distinguished man he was, and this pleased him. When he spoke with them, his voice gained strength and he offered them his charm in return for their flattery. But from time to time, he drifted into silence, which was something he had never done in my presence. It was as if what had happened to him in the bathtub had made him see his own mortality in a new dimension.

When time came for him to leave the hospital, there was no question of his riding the bus or going by the faculty club for a bloody mary. I picked him up at the hospital around eleven and we started to Sewanee. As soon as we were on the interstate, Allen began to fret about lunch. Helen had phoned him the night before and told him to be sure that we ate on the way: she would have no lunch for us. I understood why. She had two children on her hands and Allen to be put to bed and waited on as soon as we got there. Allen was embarrassed. I told him I was not hungry and that I could eat on the way home, but he was adamant. We must stop and let him buy me something. Halfway to Monteagle, we went into a Wendy's or a Burger King, which was the only sort of place we could find along the interstate. Allen waited in a booth, trying to get his breath while I bought our hamburgers.

He took one bite of his sandwich, had a sip of iced tea, and lit a cigarette. "I'm sorry this isn't better," he said. "I wish we could have found a nicer place."

"It's fine," I said. "I like hamburgers."

When I was finished we made our slow progress back to the car. Allen had insisted on paying, and I had let him. He relaxed, and we made the rest of the trip without much conversation.

Less than a year later, the Tates were in Nashville. Allen moved from the small guest room of the house in Sewanee where Helen had put him after he returned from the hospital to the small room in the house near St. Henry's Church where he dictated his correspondence and resumed his consideration of how to make money. Mort Weisman and Durrett Wagner at the Swallow Press had begun work on a new edition of *The Fathers* only to discover that the copyright had lapsed. Alan Swallow had reissued the novel in 1960, and it remained in print for several years. The copyright should have been renewed in 1966 but this was the year that Allen divorced Isabella and married Helen and about the time that Weisman was negotiating to take control of Swallow and move it to Chicago. Everyone who might have been expected to renew the copyright seems to have been diverted. The novel, as it had appeared from Putnam in 1938, passed into the public domain.

In an effort to regain ownership of the novel, Allen tried to revise it. By his own count, he made more than a hundred changes in the text, but the only one of importance was in the last paragraph. He tried to clarify the thematic significance of George Posey's role in the story, but succeeded only in stripping the book of some of the power that had been generated by the ambiguity of the original. "This new ending will be more to your liking," he said to me. "It makes the book much stronger." I think he believed this in the same way that Mr. Ransom thought he had improved his poems when he revised them in his old age. And Allen needed to believe he had improved his novel to assuage the guilt he felt over losing the copyright.

Swallow Press incorporated Allen's changes and made etchings, but they stopped production when Allen signed a contract with Farrar, Straus & Giroux for the publication of his *Collected Poems*. I do not know the details of the agreement Allen had reached with Swallow, but in the conversations he had with Mort Weisman in Chicago in 1971, the intentions on both sides seemed clear. They wanted Swallow to be Allen's publisher, and they were willing to bring out just about anything he wanted to see in print. Allen, who had fallen out with Scribner's, wanted a firm he could depend on to publish all his books. But now his need for money was more prominent in his mind than it had been then, and confined to his bed and his oxygen tank as he was, he was less a free agent. His judgments, which seemed to be heavily influenced by Helen, sometimes appeared to be penny wise and pound foolish. He began to ask large sums for permission to print quotations from his poetry and to anthologize his work; critics and editors were not always willing to pay. Allen claimed that Swallow had not sold enough of his books and answered their complaints about his contract with Farrar, Straus with demands for more money for *The Fathers*. Swallow had had enough. They tried to recoup what they had spent on *The Fathers* by selling the etchings and publication rights to the Louisiana State University Press, which brought out the new version along with two early Tate stories.

Allen was virtually bedridden by the time Helen brought him to Nashville, but his mind was still clear. He appointed Robert Buffington his biographer after what negotiations among him and Bob and Helen one can only imagine. Although Allen probably would have known better, Helen may have thought that she could control what Bob wrote and Bob may unwittingly have encouraged her in this belief by his reticence. Like the late A. J. Liebling who, it was said, conducted interviews by sitting in stony silence until his subject broke and told all, Bob feels little obligation to keep a conversation alive. In all likelihood, he said nothing while Allen and Helen told him what they expected of him, and they—or she—perhaps assumed that he was saying yes because he did not say no. However this may have been, Bob was able to get information from Allen and to fend off Helen without having bluntly to face the issue of censorship until Allen died in 1979. Then when he got word through an intermediary that he was not to include the name of Natasha Spender in his book about Allen—Stephen was teaching a term at Vanderbilt and they had heard about the biography—Bob publicly declared his independence, saying that if he left out all the names he had been pressed to leave out, there would not be much left to write.

In his last years, Allen had visitors other than Bob. He had become, as Malcolm Cowley was to say of himself later, a literary institution. Having lived through the twenties and thirties and forties, and having known most of the writers who had worked then, he could fill in gaps and offer interpretations for scholars and critics who were writing about the lives and works of his friends. Young poets and novelists, many of whom had never before met him, visited him to pay their respects. Old friends came. Howard Nemerov, who had joined in the scheme to get the Nobel Prize for Allen, added distance and time to a trip he was making somewhere else to stop in Nashville. Walker Percy and Eudora Welty visited Allen. Jesse Wills, who had been one of the Fugitives and who had resumed writing poetry after he retired from the insurance business, came bearing his own oxygen tank. Like Allen, he was stricken with emphysema. He died before Allen, and when he did, Allen fussed because Ellen, Jesse's widow, did not give Helen Jesse's automobile.

In spite of the small room, the narrow bed from which he could not rise, and the apparatus through which he breathed, Allen received his guests with grace and courtesy, but the tension under which he ordinarily lived could not be hidden. Helen was unhappy and said so to everyone who came through her door. She appeared to assume that only men were interested in talking to Allen. If a man and woman arrived together, Helen engaged the woman with her complaints of how difficult it was to care for Allen and how little money they had, and she would continue to talk to the woman until it was time for the guests to leave. If no woman were present, she would tell whoever was there her troubles, and Allen would pretend not to be embarrassed and agree with everything she said. But it was plain that her unhappiness made him unhappy and her complaints, which did not stop with the departure of the visitors, added to the discomforts that he already felt. Finally, he told Fannie Cheney that he had to escape. The circumstances under which he lived, he said, threatened his very existence.

When his condition worsened and he went into the hospital a year or eighteen months before he died, he devised a typically complex scheme to get in touch with Nancy. In earlier days, he had claimed that neither Nancy nor her family paid any attention to him, and he said that the only time he heard from Nancy was when she wanted something from him. This was not true. His grandson and namesake, Allen Wood, was a student at Sewanee in the late sixties. He visited Allen, and Allen enjoyed seeing him, though he did not quite know what to make of the way Allen looked and lived. Young Allen was a man of his time with long hair and shaggy beard, and one afternoon he spent hours telling Allen and Helen about his participation in student demonstrations at the Democratic convention in 1968. He had dodged cannisters of tear gas and climbed trees to escape the Chicago police.

But Helen and perhaps Allen continued to feel neglected by Nancy even when the evidence indicated otherwise. After Allen's collapse at Princeton in 1973, Nancy had flown with him to Nashville and driven him to Sewanee where she and Helen had argued bitterly. Nancy may not have passed through Helen's door; she certainly was not invited to stay. She telephoned Fannie Cheney from the Nashville airport. She told Fannie of her outrage at what she considered Helen's ingratitude and repeated to Fannie what she had said to her father. She was willing to take care of him, as she would care for her mother when Caroline left Dallas in 1978, but she would not be responsible for Helen and John and Benjamin. When he entered Vanderbilt Hospital in 1977, Allen believed he was ready to go to Nancy on these terms.

Allen's first concern was for secrecy. He did not want Helen to know what he was about. He chose James Patrick as his emissary to Nancy, which at first seemed a strange choice. Jim had designed Allen's house in Sewanee, and he had helped arrange for Allen to get a gold medal from Aquinas College in Nashville. He and Allen had lunch together from time to time and enjoyed each other's company, but he was not one of Allen's close friends. Jim had begun his professional life as an architect, had become an Episcopal priest, converted to Catholicism, returned to architecture, and now was moving back into theology. He divided his time between the school of architecture at the University of Tennessee in Knoxville and the philosophy department at Aquinas where Jane also taught. Allen told Jane, when she visited him, that he had to see Jim at once.

For two days, Jane left notes in Jim's mailbox and pinned to his office door with no effect. As time passed, Allen began to be frantic. He had to talk to Jim so Jim could arrange for Nancy to come and see him. He could not call Nancy himself or let his close friends call her because Helen might find out. Jim finally responded to one of Jane's notes, talked to Allen, made a previously scheduled trip to Chicago and telephoned Jane from there. Allen, whom Jim did not know intimately, wanted him to get in touch with Nancy, whom he did not know at all. Nancy, Allen thought, was in Mexico. He wanted her to stop in Nashville to see him on her way back to Princeton. Jim was to tell her this which, after a long conversation with Jane who refused to advise him, he reluctantly did. Nancy was not averse to seeing her father, but she decided to telephone him first. According to Allen, he answered his phone just as a storm broke over Nashville. "Daddo?" Nancy said. "Nancy!" Allen replied. Then there was a flash of lightning, a clap of thunder, and the line went dead.

That conversation was never resumed, but Allen remained ready to leave Nashville. In 1978, he called Nancy and asked her to bring him to a nursing home in Princeton. She told him that she and Percy and Caroline were moving to Mexico. She was willing to take him too—and Caroline was willing for him to come—but he did not want to go there. He stayed in his small room, his body growing more frail, his faculties diminishing. Blindness began in the middle of his line of vision, and spread until he could see only peripherally. He could read large print, but the sort of thing he wanted to read printed large was hard to find. He had a radio by his bed, but in spite of the fact that he had once considered becoming a professional musician and had continued to play his violin for most of his life, he did not seem much to enjoy listening to music. He began to forget names and dates and places, and he told the same stories over and over again. Even so, his mind was still impressive. The repeated anecdotes about Vanderbilt and Paris, about Archibald MacLeish and Crane and Hemingway and other people he had known and liked or not liked were still well told and interesting to listen to. His manners were still good and his powers of vituperation were barely diminished. Not long before he died, he castigated me over the phone for not inviting him to a very small party Jane and I were having for Walker Percy. Except to go to the hospital or a doctor's office, he had not been out of his house for longer than either he or I could say with certainty. "It never occurred to me that I ought to invite you," I said. "I didn't think you could come."

"I couldn't," he said testily, "but Helen could. You should have invited her."

Allen would have thought of something to say to that, but I could not. I could only apologize as if I had betrayed him.

VIII

RED AND Eleanor Warren came to Nashville for Allen's funeral. They stayed with the Cheneys, and after the burial, they and Jane and I and William T. Bandy and his wife had dinner at the table where years before Lon had said of Allen: "He's a monster, but I love him." That night we were all thinking of Allen in gentler terms, but at first we did not talk about him. Bill Bandy was a professor of French at Vanderbilt. He and Allen had met as undergraduates, and Bill had been in Paris working on his doctorate when Allen was there on his Guggenheim. Bill had attended some of Ford Madox Ford's parties to which the Tates were always invited, and Allen had been Bill's best man at his first wedding. In the intervening years, Bill had earned an international reputation as a Baudelaire scholar. That night at the Cheneys', he turned our conversation to French poetry. Or rather, he lectured us on the subject because he knew more about it than anybody else, and whenever one of us tried to say anything, he denigrated our French accents. Finally, Eleanor said, "Bill, you think you're the only person in the world who knows how to speak French." But Bill did not let this admonishment impede him. He continued his monologue that left the rest of us free to think and to remember.

Looking across the table at Red, hearing his courteous responses that allowed Bill to keep talking, I thought of how different Red was from Allen. It had been impossible for

Allen not to pass judgment. He had an opinion on just about everything anybody did—usually unfavorable. Surely, Red made judgments too, but he seldom uttered them. He once said that you could not write a novel about Robert E. Lee because Lee was "as smooth as an egg." There must have been much turmoil inside Lee, Red continued. He must have had some blood lust or he would not have been so good at his profession; but he had such "monumental self-control" that trying to write fiction about him would be like trying to write about your "sainted grandmother." Red's self-control was monumental, too. After he had returned from Oxford and married his first wife Cinina, he seemed to his friends to have withdrawn a part of himself from public observation. In their correspondence, Allen and Andrew Lytle sometimes referred to him as "the man with the iron mask." He discussed most of what happened in the world with detachment.

When I visited Red at New Haven in 1952, I met a man who had been on the faculty at LSU with him and Cleanth. The man, whose name I do not remember, was now living in New York, and he had come to Sunday dinner at the Brooks's wearing a wrinkled denim shirt and escorting a woman in long beads and a shapeless dress whose hair needed washing. The man had become a carpenter, and he and his friend were wise in the ways of the city. They talked about when and where it was safe to park an automobile and how to find work and how to deal with landlords. Being Trotskyites, they talked a lot of politics too, all of which seemed to fascinate Red and mildly fascinated Eleanor and appeared to bemuse Cleanth and Tinkum. Later Red told me that the man had once been a virtuous husband and a Democrat, but he had fallen under the influence of a philosophy professor at LSU who had started a Communist discussion group for his own amusement. When he got tired of the game, the philosopher resumed his ordinary life in the suburbs with his wife and two, as Red put it, "flaxen haired children." Except for the man I met, the other members of the cell had returned to their conventional ways, but the visitor to the Brooks's had been permanently converted. He had left his family and the academic life and now worked for revolution when he was not earning a living. His abandoned wife had responded, Red said, by joining the WACs—this had all happened at the beginning of World War II—where exercise and a sense of purpose had firmed her figure and brightened her outlook. "The last time I saw her," Red said, "she was a knockout."

This was a typical Warren story. Red laughed about it and relished the irony of it, but he drew no morals from it. Whatever he may have thought about it, or of almost any story he told, he was content to shape the material into dramatic coherence and allow it to stand for itself, though often, as with the tale of the rich man who visited him in Minneapolis, the meaning was obvious.

Allen was a good raconteur too, but he let you know at the outset who were the villains and who were the heroes, if any, and he glossed his narratives as he told them. He liked to tell about Djuna Barnes who, after a long and convivial lunch with T. S. Eliot, fell inside her own front door and could not get up. E. E. Cummings, who lived across from her—this was in New York—and who did not like her, heard her cries and came to help her. Her door was locked. Cummings found a ladder, climbed through an open window and set out to get Barnes on her feet. She was fat and drunk, and Cummings had difficulty getting a proper hold on her. Once or twice, she slipped from his grasp and landed with a thump on the floor. Finally, Cummings got his arms under hers. He set her back against the door and inched her up until she was on her feet. Allen told this story with gleeful malice and with a tone of moral superiority that suggested that nothing stronger than mother's milk had ever passed his lips. He seemed to enjoy most recounting Cummings' declaration that before he would rescue Djuna Barnes again, he would let her die where she had fallen.

This was not the sort of story that I ever heard Red tell. It was anecdotal, whereas his usually had the shape of fiction, with passages of thematic development as well as beginnings and ends. If Red had told it, he would have laughed, as

109

Allen did, but his laughter would have been charitable and his voice, as he told the story, would have been gentle. Red is a very kind man. The characters in his novels are greatly burdened by original sin and behave accordingly; but he seems to have an abundance of what theologians call natural grace—a basic instinct for generous behavior. He looks for opportunities to say nice things, to do favors, to find ways to make other people feel good about themselves. Allen could be equally kind when he wanted to be, but with Red, kindness is a habit that he seldom, if ever, abandons. This seems paradoxical in view of Allen's transcendent view, which Red has never shared.

Unlike Mr. Davidson and Mr. Ransom and to a certain extent Red Warren, Allen had not received much religious training in his youth. This may have left him free of preconceptions and more open to the instinct toward Catholicism that was evident in some of his letters and essays and poems twenty years before he was received into the church. Early in 1929, he wrote Mr. Davidson: "I am more and more headed toward Catholicism. We have reached a condition of the spirit where no further compromise is possible." In "Remarks on the Southern Religion," Tate's contribution to *I'll Take My Stand*, he claimed that the refusal to embrace Catholicism had been a major flaw in southern civilization. And the sense of incompleteness that he found in Protestantism is evident in "The Cross," which he wrote late in 1928. Jacques Maritain told him after his confirmation in 1950 that if he had delayed his entry into the church any longer, he would have been "committing a sin against the Holy Ghost." Yet his personal life seemed a poor advertisement for the Catholic faith, and he did not appear to change much during his last months.

He knew he was dying. Every day his breath grew shorter, his eyesight dimmed, his body weakened. He must have thought a great deal about death and discussed it with the priests who visited him, brought him communion, heard his confessions. But to the rest of the world, he was not much different than he had always been: aside from money, the consideration of which was forced upon him, his main interests were still literature and sex; he talked of both of them. He thought often of Caroline and remembered her fondly; he spoke admiringly of her novels; but I never heard him suggest that he regretted the heartache he had caused her. His old love affairs ran through his mind, and he would mention them. When Helen was not present, he called the names of other women as if they evoked for him a better time. He reconsidered not only his own sex life, but that of others. One afternoon he said, "Walter, I hope Don had coitus with somebody besides Theresa. I hope she wasn't the only woman he ever went to bed with."

Mr. Davidson was dead. When he was alive, he did not talk about sex except to condemn its depiction in modern literature. He taught *Sons and Lovers*, which appealed to his Agrarian principles, but he was not comfortable with the Lawrence canon and said so. He allowed no explicit love scenes in the work he received from his writing students. And he claimed that in World War I, American soldiers and in turn the American nation had been corrupted by the foul language of British troops and by French prostitutes. I am making him sound more prudish than he was; but my point is that, in my judgment, there was no chance that he would have been unfaithful to Mrs. Davidson, and almost none that he would have entered into a relationship with any woman before he was married. In this respect, he was as unlike Allen as was possible. But of course, Allen's remark was aimed at Mrs. Davidson more than at him.

She was from Ohio; she and Mr. Davidson had met in 1916 when she was teaching Greek and Latin at Martin College in Pulaski, Tennessee. When I first met her, she must have been in her forties, though she seemed older. Like Mr. Davidson, and unlike Allen and the women he pursued, she wore plain clothes, made little effort at self-beautification. She was very much under Mr. Davidson's domination. Sometimes when she tried to express an opinion, he told her to be quiet and she obeyed, though she talked intelligently when she

111

was allowed to. Still, under the best of circumstances, she would never have been a sensual woman, and nobody would have known this sooner or better than Allen. The surprise was that as he lay within months of his death, this was what he thought of. Or at least this is one of the things he thought of to say to those of us who came to his bedside.

Caroline spent her last days at Nancy's ranch in Chiapas, where she could be cared for by and end her life among Catholics of a sort she greatly admired: those of simple faith who believed all the mysteries. As she had requested, she was buried in Mexico. Because of her deep religious gifts and extraordinary singlemindedness, she was able throughout her life to concentrate on whatever possessed her mind and to survive her inner conflicts. For Allen, the inner conflicts as well as those he entered into with others, seemed to be the basis of his nature. I think when he told Red that he was the most innocent boy who had ever entered Vanderbilt, he halfway believed—in spite of his studs and his monocle—what he was saying. A part of him was, or at least always wanted to be, the well-bred, sheltered, southern boy, the provincial. But even as he cherished this role and developed out of it his novel and some of his essays and the imagery for some of his best poetry, he yearned toward a life of cosmopolitan sophistication.

In New York, he cultivated friends whose political views and personal preferences were not consonant with those he had learned in his youth and later endorsed with his participation in Agrarianism. He continued his correspondence with Mr. Davidson while he sought the company of Malcolm Cowley and lived in the same house with Hart Crane. Once he had been to Paris, a part of his loyalty was permanently captured by the best aspects of the same European culture that Mr. Davidson had seen as the corrupter of America. All this is as well known as the poems—"The Mediterranean," for example, and "Aeneas at Washington"—which proceed from a successful amalgamation of the southern and classical and modern European traditions. After Allen became a Catholic, he did not write much poetry; but another dimension was added to what he did write and another dimension was added to the divisions within himself. His belief took him one way, his concupiscence another: his soul was divided as, earlier in his life, his mind had been. He seemed during the long silences of his last illness to hover between memories of illicit pleasure and the hope of salvation. But his spirituality was real. He said more than once, "Whoever doesn't believe in God is a fool," thus paraphrasing Saint Paul and employing his habitual idiom of vituperation. But late in his life, it seemed to me that his thoughts were closing in and he was thinking more of himself and spending less of his energy condemning others.

The night of Allen's funeral, the Bandys left the Cheneys' as soon as dinner was over and left a silence behind them. The rest of us went to Lon and Fannie's library faced with the task of trying to think of something to say, because most conversation about the dead is conducted in clichés, and this would not do for Allen. We got our coffee and took our seats. We talked of people we had seen that day. Andrew had come to the funeral. Daniel Hoffman had flown down from Philadelphia and said that he could not have stayed away: Allen had meant too much to him. "Well, God bless him," Lon said at last. "He's gone." This seemed appropriate, making as it did no assessment, no judgment. Fannie solved our problem by doing what she often did when she had writers in her house: she brought Red a book and asked him to read some of his own poetry.

Red, who on other visits had brought manuscript along and read works in progress, this time stuck to poems that he knew we knew well. We could listen without effort, hearing the lines as you hear familiar music, and at the same time remember Allen. Allen had often read his own work in this room. His voice and his accent had been different from Red's. He once told me that Red had no ear for the spoken language, that he ran his words together and that the rhythms of his sentences were wrong. I thought of that and of the man in Minneapolis whom Allen said believed he talked according to nature and noted one more paradox out of the mind that had been a part of Allen Tate. On the night that Allen and Lon had had their argument about Teilhard and the Ascension, we had sat in the living room, which had been inauspicious in itself, since almost always at the Cheneys we sat in the library.

With Red's voice sounding rhythmically enough in the background of my thoughts, I remembered better times in this room: Allen on a fine October day, dressed for Sunday brunch, wearing a Paisley scarf, an ivory colored shirt, a brown jacket. He had held a bloody mary in one hand, a cigarette in the other, neither of which he should have allowed himself. On that and many other occasions, he had stood in front of the mantel and in front of the shelves that held Lon's and Fannie's books. He had sat in the chair Red was sitting in now, and he had made a thousand passages through the wide entrance hall, back to the bar and back again, a new drink in his hand, ready to plunge once more into conversation.

Allen talked. That was one of the things I remembered best about him. Except under the worst of circumstances—when he was crushed by grief or laid low by sickness—he brought to every conversation energy and wit and wisdom. After the first session of the Fugitives' reunion in May, 1956, he had sat in the old Allen Hotel and drunk Jack Daniels straight and explained to Louise Cowan, who as I remember was sipping Coca-Cola, what she doubtless already knew about Catholic theology. Indeed, there was nothing new to any of us in the facts he stated, but he was able usually to put old knowledge into new conformations as on this night he related the laws for fasting before communion not to the crucifixion or the body and blood of Christ, but to the nativity. He and Louise were talking of going to Mass the next morning at the cathedral across the street from where they were staying. I expect she got there; I know that Allen did not. But he was ready by nine o'clock to continue the reprise of the Fugitive and Agrarian years and to point out what the group had accomplished and where they had been right and where wrong and what they should have done that they had failed to do.

Early in 1969, ten years before he died, Allen asked if I would serve, along with William Jay Smith, as one of his literary executors. He wrote that the favor he was about to ask of me would occupy time I might otherwise use to pray for his soul, but he wanted to leave his literary affairs in the hands of competent people. I accepted gladly and, for about a week, I took my role as Allen's future executor seriously. I assumed that he wanted me to handle *The Fathers* and his other fiction and perhaps some of his criticism and that Bill Smith would have the more important task of dealing with his poetry. Then it occurred to me that if Allen were behaving true to form, he had probably asked others to serve as his executors before he asked Bill and me, and in all likelihood had not bothered either to change his will or to notify them of their dismissal. He would probably change his mind several times more—without telling us—before he died. But it was increasingly clear that the question of whom he would finally choose was moot: Helen would be his executor.

She would ask too much for reprint rights; she would demand that future biographers share their earnings with her—and at least one of them would accede to this request; she would ask royalties for publishing his correspondence, and, in her search for money, she would impede the study of Allen's work and the inclusion of his poems in anthologies. But this did not matter. There were enough copies of his books already in circulation to assure him of a future hearing. On the shelf behind Red, there was almost every volume Allen had published. They were all inscribed to Fannie and Lon "with love" or "with much love" or "with love more than ever." He had loved them, and they had loved him with an affection that transcended what Lon, and most of the rest of us, recognized as his capacity for monstrous behavior. He was a complicated man, but without his complications and complexities, he perhaps could not have written his criticism and his poetry. I thought that night, not for the first time, that much of the little understanding I have of literature had come from him, and I was grateful. Whatever small agonies his bad temper had caused me were nothing when weighed against the benefits of his friendship. I had been lucky to know him.

T. S. Eliot has admired him too, had praised Allen's poetry and criticism and the qualities of his mind; he had called him a "representative of the smallest of minorities, that of the intelligent who refuse to be described as 'intellectuals.' " Allen returned Eliot's affection in spite of the difference in their temperaments. Unlike Allen, Eliot tried to keep his domestic affairs private and he was careful in his conversation not to disclose too much of himself. But he was Christian and conservative and, as Allen frequently recalled, he kept a picture of the Pope on his desk. Once when Allen was visiting Eliot at John Hayward's apartment, the phone rang, and Hayward, who often made acerbic remarks, said, "Don't answer it. It's probably just another American poet."

"Well," Eliot replied, "in that case I'd *better* answer it, because I'm half American myself."

Much later in his office at Faber and Faber, Eliot expressed to Allen his sorrow that Allen and Caroline were "no longer together." He told Allen that in marriage there had to be "giving from both sides; both parties had to offer something of themselves."

In his last years, when his mind was on the past, Allen often repeated this comment, considering, perhaps, what he and Caroline had withheld from each other. "Writers should never marry other writers," he told me once. Maybe he was right. He and Caroline were apart. Cal Lowell and Jean Stafford had long been divorced. Of the three literary couples who had spent Easter weekend with the Tates in 1943, only Peter and Eleanor Taylor remained together. Allen clearly wished that his own married life had been different, but he seemed not to know how, if he could live it again, he would change it.

He lay in bed and thought and to the end of his days he viewed his own behavior with a kind of innocence. In 1957, Caroline, still deeply hurt by her separation from Allen, consented to spend Christmas at Smyrna with the Cheneys. Fannie, not knowing that the Tates were estranged, invited Allen too and put him and Caroline in the same bedroom. The Cheneys called their house Idlers Retreat, but its builders had named it Cold Chimneys. On the first night of their Christmas visit, Allen apparently expected Caroline to be more cordial than she was. "Fannie and Lon should have kept the name Cold Chimneys," he told her, "because tonight it's mighty cold in here." He always expected to be forgiven and usually he was.

Now, in the Cheneys' library, Red finished a poem and closed his book. We all stood as if on cue. Red and Eleanor were leaving the next morning; Jane and I told them goodby and said how glad we'd been to see them. This brought us back to why they had come—back to Allen.

Another silence fell.

"Well" Lon said, repeating himself, "he's gone. He's gone. God bless him."

We all nodded and agreed, solemnly, as if the fact of his death required our validation. Then we said goodnight, and Jane and I drove back to Nashville.